5/14/96

HATE is TENACIOUS
MEMORY is FRAGILE.

Joseph Houy

MARK IT WITH A STONE

MARK IT WITH A STONE

Joseph Horn

BARRICADE BOOKS
New York

Published by Barricade Books Inc.
150 Fifth Avenue
New York, NY 10011

Printed in the United States of America.

Library of Congress Cataloging-in-Publication Data

Horn, Joseph, 1926-
    Mark it with a stone / by Joseph Horn.
        p.   cm.
    ISBN 1-56980-068-5 (Cloth)
    1. Jews—Poland—Radom (Radom)—Persecutions. 2. Holocaust,
Jewish (1939-1945)—Poland—Radom (Radom)—Personal narratives.
3. Horn, Joseph, 1926- . 4. Radom (Radom, Poland)—Ethnic relations.
I. Title.
    DS135.P62R318 1996
    940.53′18′092—dc20
    (B)   95-51075
                                                 CIP

First Printing

To the memory of

the victims of the Holocaust

who (silently) command us

to remember.

ACKNOWLEDGMENTS

No post-war task was as daunting as writing this Holocaust memoir. To re-live those terrible days and re-visit the abominimal places is impossible without tremendous motivation. For that, I thank my NYU teacher, Marion Landew, my editor David King, my wife Dinah, and my daughters, Sandra Rubenstein, Bonnie Adler and Ellen Blumen.

FOREWORD

The day I walked off the troop ship *Marine Marlin* when it docked in New York City on March 3, 1947, a newly arrived United States immigrant, I was interviewed by a representative of the Jewish Joint Distribution Committee, the sponsor of my visa. The interviewer was a seemingly well-meaning young lady, full of compassion and eagerness to help, who spoke Yiddish with a smattering of English. Her first question was about the brown manila envelope I clutched under my arm.

"It's a manuscript," I said. "It describes my experiences in the concentration camps."

Her face went blank, and she gave a dismissive motion with her arm. "Oh, another one of those."

With hindsight, I can hardly blame her for her lack of interest in another account of a tale that already seemed terribly exaggerated and impossible to believe. This was a time when America was listening to the firsthand, authentic, wartime experiences of their own sons and daughters. Books were being published with factual accounts of heroic feats in faraway, exotic places. Hollywood was busy filming war movies with genuine American heroes, all historically accurate, all with happy endings. America had undertaken the task of preserving democracy and decency in the world and succeeded beyond anyone's expectations. Never did America seem more righteous, more decent, more moral, than at the end of World War II. It was a time to rejoice, a time to mourn the fallen heroes, and a time to begin a new era.

How could my story upstage these powerful emotions of pride and accomplishment, especially given what my story was. The newsreels about the liberation of the concentration camps then being shown in local theaters were so gruesome and unbelievable that most people—including the American Jewish community—simply could not take in the story. So although the Nazis singled out Jews for total extinction in Europe and committed the most heinous atrocities against them, there was relatively little understanding or sympathy in America for the survivors. People were not yet ready to listen.

In 1964, I applied to the German restitution office in Stuttgart for compensation on the basis that I had been shattered psychologically and physically by my Holocaust experiences. I was interviewed and examined extensively by several German doctors assigned by the restitution office. They agreed that I was traumatized as an adolescent and emotionally impaired and recommended a small monthly stipend. The doctor's report went to a three-judge restitution court in Stuttgart and was summarily rejected. No human being, ruled the court, is capable of withstanding the experiences which I described, therefore, they concluded, I must be lying. They were not yet ready to believe. Or perhaps they didn't want to believe.

Historians have studied the Holocaust exhaustively. Analysts have written extensive volumes of material on the events themselves. Theologians and philosophers have made innumerable efforts to make this event comprehensible to the enlightened minority that cares. Yet, the more one knows about it, the less one understands. The truth of the Holocaust threatens the most cherished human instincts. How do you comprehend an event that asks if you would be able to give up your child to prolong your own life, albeit temporarily?

Even survivors of the Holocaust who have seen the horrors of Nazi Germany firsthand are often of no help in conveying them to others. They do not understand the horrors themselves. In fact, the Nazis' greatest asset in engineering the Holocaust was their victims' inability to comprehend the scope of brutality that one human being was intent on inflicting upon another in this supposedly enlightened twentieth century. How do you apply normal standards of behavior to situations beyond the comprehension of those involved? How do you tell this story so it can be understood?

And yet the story must be told and told again, especially now that an increasing number of people, some well known with large political followings such as Pat Buchanan, openly question the eyewitness accounts of survivors like myself. More and more, we hear the refrain, "enough already," not only from those who hate us but also from allies who have the ostrich mentality, who will hear no evil and see no evil. If we no longer talk or write about the Holocaust, we will be handing over a great victory to our deadliest enemies, past, present, and future.

Now that Germany has been reunited, there are some all-too-familiar rumblings emanating from that nation. If nations were to be judged like individuals for crimes they committed, no impartial jury would ever give Germany another chance at freedom. But our leaders have short memories. When President Ronald Reagan put wreaths on the graves of fallen German soldiers of the Second World War at an SS cemetery in Bitburg, he practically absolved them of the guilt for their crimes against humanity. It seemed once more, we had learned nothing.

And so I will tell my story.

Some prominent Jewish authors, such as Isaac Bashevis Singer, wrote beautifully about prewar Eastern European Jewry but did not write about the Holocaust. I once heard Singer explain that he would not write about the Holocaust because he never wrote about anything that he did not witness. For some survivors who chose to write their stories, such as Elie Wiesel, the Holocaust did not begin until the spring of 1944 with the deportation to Auschwitz. But by that time, Nazi Germany had already committed perhaps 80 percent of the genocide against the Jewish people.

For me, the Holocaust began the first day of September 1939 when at the age of twelve, I saw the first tree-level attacks by Nazi Stukas. It ended on April 15, 1945, when the clocks stopped in Bergen-Belsen at 9:15 a.m. and I saw the first Allied armored vehicle with the five-pointed white star arrive to liberate the survivors. On that day, I swore to record what I witnessed. Jews are traditionally poor at exacting vengeance, but we have an excellent historical memory. I wanted to contribute to that memory bank.

But it is not easy. Although I have spoken to audiences and published articles about certain aspects of my experiences, I have never, since my arrival in the United States, tried to write a comprehensive account of my survival. Indeed, many of the events that follow in these pages are unknown to my children. I always felt that there was something so sacred about the extermination of so many innocent people that the mere act of telling the story was sacrosanct. For that reason, I tried to limit my conversations about my experiences to the very few of my friends whom I felt were genuinely interested. Like Art Spiegelman's father, an Auschwitz survivor whose wartime experiences were depicted in cartoon form by his son in *Maus One* and *Maus Two*, I have been able to talk about the Holocaust only to people who listen with respect to the memory of the victims.

Still, this memoir is my chance to point an accusing finger at my oppressors and to record what is indelibly marked in the inner recesses of my mind. I was a witness to the destruction of six million Jewish men, women, and children, and it is time for me to leave a record and a legacy of the crimes I have seen. To the dehumanization of the Jewish population. To the systematic infliction of constant terror and total denigration. To the inversion of civilization's sacred values by a demented leader at the head of a nation which was traditionally in the vanguard of Christian western morality. To the armband with the Jewish Star, the yellow patch, the ghettos where the victims were slowly starved to death, the "deportations," a euphemism for a one-way trip to the gas chambers. To Blizyn. Auschwitz/Birkenau. Lieberose. Peenemunde. Bergen-Belsen.

The human spirit must be Godly, for I have since managed to make a new life for myself. I have a wife, three married daughters, and four grandchildren. And I love the United States. Even though I may not express my patriotism by flying the American flag on the Fourth of July or by marching in parades, I have a deep and abiding sense of gratitude for the sacrifices this country has made in the past and continues to make to this day for the cause of freedom throughout the world.

Still, there is never a time when I play with my grandchildren that I don't think of the "other children." There is never a time when I meet my friends' parents that I don't think of my own parents and the circumstances of their demise. When I am introduced to someone, socially or professionally, I immediately assign him a place in the camp hierarchy: collaborator, duplicitous, or trustworthy and reliable. Whenever I meet someone, I wonder how he would stand up under real pressure.

Like Samson in the temple of the Philistines, I implore God to give me the strength to do justice to those we left behind. To tell their story and mine so it may touch the hearts of people, now and in the future. To make sure, to the extent that I can, that our ordeal will not have been in vain.

CHAPTER 1

BEFORE

Radom, where I was born and raised, was a city of eighty thousand located in central Poland, about sixty miles directly south of Warsaw. Back then, it was an industrial hub known mostly for its leather tanneries, although the city also manufactured textiles, steel, wood products, and china. In addition, many of the products over which the government held a monopoly such as tobacco, alcohol, matches, and sugar were either manufactured or distributed in Radom. The government also built and operated a weapons production facility that was one of the largest in the country.

In the 1930s, Jews comprised about one-third of the city's population. Because of discrimination, they held none of the well-paid government jobs. There were Jews in the professions, but they were becoming fewer and fewer as it became more and more difficult for Jews to gain admission to the universities. As a result, most Jews eked out a living as small shopkeepers, tailors, cobblers, and small entrepreneurs. But despite their position at the bottom of society, Jews were singled out in Poland as scapegoats for the widespread poverty brought on by the worldwide depression. This was further exacerbated by the xenophobic, chauvinistic, pro-Fascist, military junta in control of the government. Poland's constitution, an impressive document similar to that of the United States, theoretically gave rights to all, but the dispensation of justice was left to biased courts and bigoted, unjust police departments. The condition of Jews in Poland in the 1930s could be compared to the African-Americans in the rural South in the heyday of the Ku Klux Klan.

Under these conditions I was born, the youngest of four. My brother Abram was born in 1920. Bluma, my sister, was born in 1921. Eli was born in 1923, and I in 1926. My father's name was Judah and my mother's Yohevet.

My paternal grandfather, Abram, died before I was born, but I remember my grandmother, Yita, who died in the early thirties. My father had three brothers, Hershel, Layzor, and Maylech, and one sister, Tsipora. They were all married and lived in Radom with their extended families.

My mother was born in Pionki, a small town about twenty miles from Radom, to Koppel and Frayndl Weinberg. Grandmother Frayndl died before I was born. Grandfather Koppel lived in Pionki until his death in 1937.

My mother had an older sister, Tsyvia, an older brother, Noah, and a younger brother Mordechai. Tsyvia married a Grossfeld and lived in Radom with her husband Aron-Meyer and four children. Noah lived in Pulavy with his wife Guta and five children, and Mordechai lived in Warsaw with his wife Tosia and two children.

A strong bond of culture and tradition held my entire family together. Each member was aware of his or her standing in the community and felt duty bound to uphold the good name of the whole family. Each member of the family had an obligation to provide other members with financial or emotional support in times of need.

As I grew up, I learned that this family interconnectedness extended in its own way to the entire Jewish community.

The first rule I learned was never to strike back when hit by a Catholic child. Doing so could start a pogrom. Collective responsibility grew out of the threat of collective punishment. It followed the well-established Jewish tradition of survival at any cost until redemption and the arrival of the Messiah.

My earliest recollection is of the day when my father took me for a long walk to the city park. I was recovering from a serious illness at the time, and I believe the doctor told my parents I needed to be out in the fresh air. Certainly I recall feeling important because I had my father all to myself.

As we walked, he held me by my hand and answered all my impossible questions.

My father was a tall man, with a dark complexion and steel gray eyes. His almost gray hair was always immaculately cut and combed back without a part, and he was always clean shaven. He walked with a slight stoop as if he carried the burden of the world on his shoulders. He wore gray sharkskin suits, a lighter weight in spring and summer, and heavier woolen in the winter. His name, as I said, was Judah, and in my eyes he was a lion of a man.

When we reached the park, he stopped to look at a rectangular mark on the gate. Clearly there had been a sign there once, which had since been removed. I noticed that his eyes became glazed and a sudden sadness came over him.

"Papa, why are you so sad?" I asked.

He pulled me past the gate and into the beautiful park, then he bought me an ice-cream cone and tried to talk about the beauty of nature all around us. But like a curious child, I refused to let go of the question. Finally we sat down on a bench, and he waited until I finished my ice cream. He then explained that the city of Radom had once been occupied by Czarist Russia. During that time, the authorities affixed a sign on the gate, and when a Polish interim government was established under the Versailles Treaty, the sign was removed. But the marks were still there.

I never forgot the words which my father spoke slowly that day, first in Russian, then in Yiddish. "Jews and dogs are forbidden to enter this park."

The building in which we lived was home to more than twenty families: several Polish Catholics, the rest Jewish. Across a wide yard was another building which housed eight more Jewish families. For the most part, there was an uneasy peace between the Jews and the Poles, but there was always a cultural and religious undercurrent that separated the two.

On either side of the yard, to complete a rectangle, were wooden structures that served as garages or stables for horses and wagons. Several families who lived in this complex were in the transportation business and used these stables as needed, which meant that, when the weather was good, there was a great deal going on in our yard. Goods were being loaded or unloaded or transferred from one wagon to another, carriages came and went, horses were fed and tended. Some of my favorite memories are of Friday afternoons when we children were allowed to ride the horses bareback to the smith to have their shoes checked.

One bright, crisp, sunny morning, I lay in bed, wide awake and looking forward to a day of play and fun with my friends. The rest of the family was still asleep, and I did not dare make noise for fear of waking them. Then I heard movement in the yard. Quietly, I slipped out of bed and stuck my head out the window.

I saw a neighbor of ours, Moshke Dorozkarz (Moshke, the coachman), come into the yard as he did every morning except Saturdays and holidays to get his horse and carriage out of the stable to start his business day. That day, when he got to the stable door, he found it blocked by some clothing hung out to dry. I could see that Moshke was agitated because, after all, the clothes might belong to one of the non-Jewish families. He discreetly began to knock at windows and ask to whom the clothes belonged. At the third window, Moshke was told that the clothes belonged to Pani Raykowska, a Catholic Pole.

I knew the Raykowski family. Pan Raykowski was a confirmed alcoholic, and Pani was a nagging shrew. Their two older sons were out of school, unemployed, and already had drinking problems. And their youngest son, Zbigniew, was my contemporary and my nemesis. Even as a six year old, he knew that he could lord it over the Jewish kids, abuse them, and get away with it. I feared and hated him from the day I can remember being conscious of my Jewishness.

When Moshke found out who the clothesline belonged to, he began pacing back and forth in front of the inaccessible stable murmuring something to the effect that he needed his horse and buggy to earn a living for his wife and children. At one point, he looked up at the sky and, in the inimitable, age-old Jewish way of conversing with the Almighty, lifted his hands to the heavens and asked, "Why are you doing this to me?"

By this time, windows were wide open all around the yard. Everyone was anxiously awaiting the outcome of this unfolding drama. At last, Moshke mustered enough nerve to knock at Pani Raykowska's basement window and ask, in a pleading voice, if she would please come up and remove the clothesline so he could get his horse and buggy. There was no response. After a short interval, he knocked again, this time a bit louder, and said that as soon as he got his horse and buggy, Pani Raykowska could put the clothesline back in the same place, and he would not even mind.

The window opened and out popped Pani Raykowska's head, spewing anti-Jewish epithets. From her abuse alone, you could get a pretty good collection of anti-Semitic diatribes, starting from the two-thousand-year-old accusation of Deicide, to the more recent Beilis Affair—in which he was accused of killing Gentile children to use their blood to make Matzo—and ending with rhymed insults such as, "*Beduiny won do Palestyny*"("Bedouins out to Palestine!") and

"*Wasze kamienice ale nasze ulice*" ("You own the buildings but the streets are ours").

All Moshke could do in the face of this verbal torrent was lift his hands to the heavens and ask, "Dear God, did it have to be Pani Raykowska, the worst Jew hater of all?"

As if in response to his plea, I could clearly hear in the morning quiet the singing voice of Pan Raykowski returning from a night of drinking on the town. As the singing became louder, Pani Raykowska came up from the basement to continue her harangue, warning that when her husband arrived he would mete out just punishment to this loathsome Jew who dared disturb her peace.

The drama climaxed when Pan Raykowski entered the courtyard and, through an alcoholic haze, slowly became acquainted with the problem at hand. On one side, his wife, in a frenzy egged him on to break the Jew's bones for insulting her and for daring to disturb her peace. On the other side, Moshke stood shaking his head and repeating, "All I want to do is to get my horse and buggy so I can earn bread for my family. What's wrong with that?"

Then the unbelievable happened. Pan Raykowski's already ruddy face turned purple with rage. He turned to his wife. "*Ty stara kurwa* [you old whore]," he screamed. "This poor man has to get up early because he has to work to feed his family, not like you, you lazy bitch." In a drunken rage, he ripped the clothesline off and ordered his wife to take her rags and hang them elsewhere.

A chorus of approval and applause greeted him from the open windows. My brother Eli, always the wise guy, shouted, "Bravo Solomon." Pan Raykowski actually took his hat off and bowed like an actor on a stage.

I have remembered this incident all my life, when a Polish Catholic actually sided with a Jew. I remember it because it was an exception, the only exception I know in the unhappy life of Jews in the Polish Diaspora. In the end, such small victories as Moshke's helped lull the Jewish community into a false sense of security for which it eventually paid the ultimate price.

In the early thirties, when I was five or six, I was introduced to a *cheder*, a kind of a kindergarten school, where most Jewish children of my generation began the study of religious dogma. My mentor and teacher in the *cheder* was Rabbi Abush whom, because he had a red flaming beard, everyone called "the red rabbi."

When my mother first brought me to *cheder* to make the arrangements, Rabbi Abush seemed polite and reasonable. The school itself consisted of three classrooms strung out like railroad cars with a small office in the front vestibule. The first room held the youngest group, and the last room held the oldest. My brother, Eli, studied in the middle room—he was about eight or nine at the time. I was eager to stay because, as I looked around, I saw that most of the boys in my room were my friends. I thought it would be fun.

I asked to be seated next to Nathan, the son of our neighbors Isaac and Leah with whom I loved to play in the yard. It did not take long for Nathan to disabuse me of the notion of having fun in *cheder*. He warned me of Rabbi Abush's temper and advised me to go to another *cheder* even if it was further away. I told Nathan that I was afraid to even mention it to my mother.

My first day was devoted to learning the Hebrew alphabet from a printed page that was so old and crumpled, I was afraid it might disintegrate just by my looking at it. For the first time, I felt confined and regimented. And Rabbi Abush changed almost immediately from the smiling and polite mentor of our first meeting in my mother's presence to a strict, demanding, short-tempered autocrat.

He led us with an iron hand as we learned by rote, chanted prayers, recited passages from the Bible and memorized important excerpts. Each day I was expected to remember and recite everything I had learned the day before. We learned everything in Hebrew, which was completely foreign to me. And somehow Rabbi Abush always seemed to be behind *me* as we swayed and recited in unison hour after hour after hour. When my attention wandered for a moment, I was brought back to reality by Rabbi Abush's firm hand across the back of my neck or by a simple old-fashioned ear pull. I soon had second thoughts about the whole project, and one day I suggested to my mother that I had had enough of Rabbi Abush and his *cheder*.

In a no-nonsense voice, she said, "You will do as you are told and continue religious school."

From the vehemence of her answer, I realized that I was stuck with Rabbi Abush and would have to make the best of it.

There were certain aspects of the Bible, such as the story of Joseph and how he was sold into slavery by his brothers, that caught our imagination. At such times, the power and the beauty of the Bible seemed so great that we loved what we learned in spite of Rabbi Abush. But for the most part, the only thing I learned from the *cheder* was a distaste for religious education.

My *cheder* career came to an abrupt end one day when my middle brother, Eli, actually hit back at one of the rabbis in his classroom. Both of us were declared unfit and banned from the *cheder*. My mother endured a certain amount of shame from her peers, and my brother endured his share of reprimands from my mother, but among our friends, we were heroes.

After he had received what my parents considered enough threats and reprimands, my brother started private grade school, where he continued taking religion as one of the subjects. As for me, my mother engaged a *Melamed*, a tutor, who came to the house three times a week to keep me religiously indoctrinated. My new teacher's name was Reb Mendel. He was very tall and awkward and walked with the support of a cane. He had high cheekbones, a long, bearded face, and a relaxed manner. He wore the prescribed visored black Chassidic cap and a frayed and shiny black coat, called a "capote." His shirt was white, without a collar and buttoned all the way up to the neck.

For our first lesson, Reb Mendel tested my knowledge of the elementary prayers and my reading and writing skills and concluded that he had to start from scratch.

Every time Reb Mendel came to the house, my mother served him a giant portion of steaming hot soup with a hefty slice of buttered rye bread. He would assign some work for me while he went about sipping soup and dipping bread.

I watched his high cheekbones move up and down with a crunching rhythm as he ate with astonishing enjoyment. He always left a little bread so he could wipe the soup plate clean. When he was finished eating, he would take his tattler, a guider that looked like a pencil without lead, and start me off on that week's Bible reading. At first the tattler was firm in his hand, and it would stop when the reading was faulty, then continue firmly when I corrected myself. But after a while, the tattler began to meander across the lines. I learned to continue my reading chant uninterrupted until Reb Mendel was sound asleep.

All in all, Reb Mendel was a great improvement over the fiery red Abush.

But of course, my education, religious and otherwise, could not stop with Reb Mendel. My mother was proud of her family lineage which she traced back to important rabbinic scholars. She was vehement and uncompromising in her quest to keep our home strictly religious. One of the memories I cherish to this day is the ritual of lighting the Sabbath candles. My mother would gather all of us in a most beautiful and solemn ceremony, light the candles, and bless the family with all the strength and conviction of her abiding faith in the God of Israel.

My father, although lukewarm about religion, was very clear about education. For him education was a way to rise above the trap Polish anti-Semitism held us in. I often remember him watching me play soccer with other kids. I felt so proud when I did well when he watched me. But inevitably he would pat me on the head and say something like, "Why don't you go upstairs and study or read a book. Kicking a ball will get you nowhere."

And so, since education was of paramount importance, and since as Jews it was difficult for us to attend public schools, our parents enrolled the four of us in private schools. The expense was enormous for a family depending on one breadwinner, but the sacrifice was deemed to be worth it.

Needless to say, our parents expected us to be scholastic superachievers. My mother was a master in the subtle art of praising achievement. Every time she went out, she always managed to bring back a tale of some child who had won an academic prize or was able to recite passages from the Talmud at the age of six.

I regret to say I came to dislike these brilliant children, whom I never met. I loved to play with friends and often "forgot" to do my homework. At school I improvised as best I could, but the results were dismal. I barely scraped by. Often my mother lashed out at my lack of enthusiasm and my ingratitude, and when my father protected me (probably because I was the youngest), she accused him of spoiling me. I felt like a traitor to the family cause.

On occasion, my father would take me and my brother Eli to a bathhouse. Most Jewish people used the ritual bathhouse called "mikvah," but my father was a notch above that and considered it avant-garde to use the newly built public baths instead. For me the evening was a beautiful and memorable experience.

We met at my father's office warehouse which gave me a glimpse of the mysterious world of business he was a part of. I was impressed with the high stacks of leather in many colors lining the walls of the warehouse. I asked many questions about business and about how it was transacted. My father was always patient and informative. We then started our walk to the bathhouse with me proudly holding his hand.

The highlight of the bathing ritual was the hot sauna after which my father trained a cold-water hose on us. My father would hose us down, at first with a spray. He would gradually increase the water pressure until we squealed with delight. After that we would get wrapped in large luxurious towels and enter a dark room full of cots for a short nap. I remember always being so excited that sleep eluded me, but I knew that I had to be quiet and not disturb the others sleeping in the room.

The best of such an evening was yet to come. After we got dressed, we were ravenously hungry. Our next stop was a delicatessen restaurant called "Reshke's."

We were seated at one of the tables, and a waiter came to get the order. For us, the menu was always the same. My father ordered a batch of frankfurters called "parowki" and a plateful of fresh sliced rye bread. The waiter then brought an aluminum pot filled with water. It had an electrical cord which he plugged into a receptacle on the wall under the table. He also brought mustard, sauerkraut, and chicken fat. When the water in the pot started boiling, the bread and frankfurters appeared.

Then came an unforgettable eating experience. The frankfurters were thrown into the boiling water and after a proper interval fished out and consumed with rye bread smeared with chicken fat and mustard and sauerkraut heaped on top.

I often conjured up the memory of those meals in later years when hunger was my steady companion.

Those were far better memories than the one from the beautiful spring day when I was about ten. I found myself in front of the school, horsing around with friends, feeling a great reluctance to start classes. As on many previous occasions, a classmate suggested that we play hooky and go to the city park instead. Another boy I liked was willing to join us, and for the moment it seemed like a good idea.

We spent the day in the sun playing and having fun as only ten-year-old boys can. On the way home, I decided to stop at a stationery store near the school to buy some supplies. The store was owned by a neighbor who told me that my mother had been in the store that day to say hello. I got what I needed, signed for it, and left with a courteous good-bye.

Once outside I began to cry. Our house was quite far from the school, and my mother would never come to that side of town without visiting it. The jig was up, and my life was over. But I did not want to be late for dinner. That would just make things worse—in our house being late for dinner was almost as bad as being truant. So, head hanging low, I walked home to face the consequences.

I later learned that, when my homeroom teacher saw my mother that day, she had greeted her warmly and told her how nice it was for her to come to school to explain my absence. My mother caught on quickly, nodded in agreement, and made an excuse for me. That afternoon when I opened the door and my mother saw my terrified face, she concluded that I had already punished myself enough. Her only comment was, "I hope this experience has taught you a lesson you will never forget."

I didn't fully understand the importance of education until the summer of 1938, when my family vacationed in the small town of Pionki, near Radom, where my grandfather owned a substantial piece of land and a large house. After grandfather Koppel passed on in 1937, part of the house had been rented out and part was kept for our family and my aunt Tsyvia's family to use for vacations.

My father came out on Friday afternoons for the weekend. Every Friday afternoon, I waited for him at the Pionki train station. The anticipation of his arrival and seeing him alight from the train remains to this day one of my fondest memories. I would buy a newspaper at the station kiosk and read it carefully so we could talk about world news on our walk home.

There was much to talk about. Nazi Germany was rearming at a frantic pace. Chamberlain and Daladier were playing the appeasement game with Herr Hitler, and England issued a "White Paper" denying Jews the right to go to Palestine. Polish hooligans were throwing stink bombs into Jewish business establishments and otherwise preventing people from shopping in Jewish stores. When these practices were challenged in the Polish courts, the ruling was the infamous "Owszem," declaring that such picketing was legal. Polish-born Jews were being booted out of Germany and sent to Zbonszyn, a Polish-German border town. America was in a deep economic depression, politically isolationist, with a Nazi-supporting group called the German-American Bund marching in the streets with swastika banners flying high.

As I discussed all those events with my father, he remained an optimist.

"Jewish people have had to endure Hamans throughout history, and somehow we survived," he said. "Hitler is just another Haman. He will exact a toll, but in the long run, we will persevere."

"But father, why is the whole world against us? Why is there so much hatred? Can't we do something to defend our rights? And why can't we leave this God-forsaken place full of hatred and bigotry?"

He would pat my head, and his eyes would become sad. "To leave now would require a lot of money that we don't have. Besides, how can we leave our place of birth where everyone knows us, our friends, our relatives? The little we have here sustains us, and it is more than we can hope for in a new country in these times of depression.

"But how can we stay?"

"By relying on our faith and in our Bible. Remember, we are the people of the book."

"But what if that is not enough?"

"That is why we are trying to establish a state in Palestine. And, who knows, if not in my lifetime then perhaps in yours that will become a reality."

One day, while walking home from the railroad station, he gave me some very good news. One of the Jewish soccer teams from Radom, the "Hapoel," was scheduled to play the Polish team in Pionki the following Sunday. I loved to play soccer and loved to watch it played. Two of my cousins, twins, played striker on the "Hapoel." All week, that upcoming match was the first thing I thought of when I woke each morning. I even arranged with my mother to have a basket of goodies to hand out to my cousins and the others at halftime.

The day of the event finally came. I was at the stadium ahead of everybody. I watched the bus with the Radom players pull in and was very proud of the healthy-looking Jewish young men getting off. I greeted my cousins and showed them the basket that mother had filled with lemons, apples, strawberries, and a jar of lemonade wrapped in a towel to keep it cool. When it was time to play ball, the Jewish team took the field dressed in blue-and-white jerseys and lined up in the center of the ballpark.

My heart sank when the spectators greeted them with hisses and anti-Semitic catcalls. Then the Polish home team ran out dressed in red and white, and the cheers were deafening.

Play began, and within five minutes, the Hapoel team scored. Because I was surrounded by Poles, I was afraid to cheer, but still it felt so good inside. As if to confirm my happiness, they scored another goal within minutes. By halftime, the score stood at 2-0.

I took my basket of goodies and ran to the Jewish side, where I quickly distributed my treasure trove. I was a kid in the company of big boys, and nobody paid much attention to me except my two cousins. As I milled among the players, I sensed a lack of excitement. They seemed strangely subdued for a team with a solid halftime lead.

When the whistle blew and it was time to go back on the field, one of my cousins leaned over and whispered in my ear, "Go home now, we are going to lose."

I was stunned and didn't move. As he ran onto the field, he turned and motioned again for me to go home.

Then I understood. They had to throw the game to avoid a massacre, and he didn't want me to see their defeat.

I walked home, my spirit completely crushed. Somehow the precariousness of being Jewish sunk in at that moment more deeply than ever before. For the first time, I knew what it was to be a stranger in my homeland. I knew now that my parents were right when they set high standards of achievement for us. Prejudice against Jews was the fuel that gave the incentive for scholastic excellence. Just being good was not good enough if you were Jewish.

That afternoon on the way home from that soccer game, I became fully committed to Zionism. I decided to fight hatred and bigotry for the rest of my life, wherever it raises its ugly head. In this I never wavered, even though the struggle was about to become harder then I could possibly have imagined.

CHAPTER 2

WAR AND OCCUPATION

The summer of 1939 had come and gone. The annual vacation in Pionki was over, and I was glad to be in Radom again. I was back with my city friends and looking forward to entering high school. Not only was I taking more of an interest in my education after the soccer incident the previous summer, but this year I was going to be able to wear the school insignia, which was a great leap toward adulthood. The problem was that the insignia—a shoulder patch and matching cap—were not mandatory, and it was hard to justify spending a considerable amount of money on a nonessential.

I remember meeting one of my schoolmates who had already managed to get his school patch sewn on the left sleeve of his navy blue jacket. He also sported a visor cap with a matching patch—the number 411, sewn in white embroidery on a pale blue background. I invited my friend to our house and introduced him to my mother so that she could see the beautiful uniform, and in his presence, I asked her for the money to buy one of my own. This was not fair, I knew, but I wanted this uniform badly.

To my great surprise, my mother barely protested.

I saw the proud, approving look in her eyes. This stoic, beautiful woman could not afford to spend money nonsensically, but it was impossible for her to refuse my earned joy. I was then twelve years old and due to enter high school on September 1, 1939.

It was on September 1, 1939, that the first German bombs rained down on Warsaw. We heard the heavy bomb-laden Heinkels pass overhead early that morning on their mission of destruction.

The following day, Saturday, a few bombs hit Radom. Then, for the next seven days until Friday, September 8, we were subjected to daily bombardment either by heavy Heinkel bombers or by diving Stukas. The Stuka attacks were the worst. They came down on us with a terrifying noise, the pitch increasing until they were within a few hundred yards of the target, when they dropped the bombs. Then they pulled up and came around again.

The Luftwaffe bombing had nothing to do with war strategy. It was simply used as a tool to terrorize and panic the people. Thousands of innocent civilians were killed on the clogged roads, when they left their homes to seek safety in the countryside. On the second day of the war, I watched three Stuka dive bombers kill our milkman, his two boys, and the three cows they owned, as they were grazing in a nearby meadow. For the pilots, this massacre was just target practice. After seven days of terror, everyone pleaded for an end to the nightmare, no matter what the consequences.

On Friday the eighth of September at about four in the afternoon, I saw a German plane fly over the city from west to east and release an orange flare to signify that the city was ready to be entered by their ground forces. Then I heard a mighty rumble coming in from the west and curiosity overcame fear. I went to the road towards the rumble and for the first time saw the mighty German army. As I watched with my hands clasped over my head, I was awestruck by the raw power generated by each passing tank. They came by the scores, endlessly, and I knew that nothing would ever be the same again. As I looked at the dust-covered, goggled tankers, I thought I was watching a movie unfold on a screen—they seemed so powerful, God-like in their majestic glory. All I could think of was, Why couldn't I be part of such might?

As I was standing with my hands on my head, a motorcycle with a sidecar pulled up and stopped in front of me. Two German officers were seated on the cycle. The sidecar was empty. They were in battle gear, wearing goggles, which made them look like creatures from Mars.

Presently one of them asked, "*Wo ist ein beckerei?* [Where is a bakery?]"

It was easy for me to understand because of the connection between Yiddish and German. I offered to take them.

And so I got my first ride in a German vehicle on the first day of occupation. I brought them to the nearest bakery where they bought a five-pound rye bread for fifty-five groschen and made me keep the change from a five-zloty bill. They were courteous, friendly, and very much surprised at the easy availability of such freshly baked, tasty bread. They departed waving a friendly good-bye.

I could not wait to get home to share my good fortune with the family and also to reassure them that the Germans were not all that bad.

Of course, we were forewarned repeatedly about Nazi hatred of Jews. We read about the brutalities of Nazi concentration camps like Dachau, Buchenwald, and Sachsenhausen and brooded over the atrocities of *Kristallnacht*. But despite all of this, the Jewish community in Poland was not at first greatly alarmed by the German victory. There were two reasons.

First, my parents' generation remembered the German occupation of Radom in the First World War when the Germans were considered liberators from Czarist Russian oppression. The Germans brought the first winds of enlightenment to Poland. They were remembered for their culture, good behavior, excellent administration, and even-handed justice.

Second, by the late thirties, the pitch of Polish anti-Semitism had increased to the point that Jews believed almost any change would be for the better. For instance, just before the war, there was a pogrom in Przytyk, a suburb of Radom. Afterwards, the Gentile perpetrators who had murdered several Jews were tried in the Radom district court and released with suspended sentences. The Jews who defended themselves were given long jail sentences.

In the minds of the Jews of Poland of that period, the Poles were as much a threat as the Germans. Because our parents retained a positive image of the Germans from the First World War, they were hoping against hope that the German occupation would somehow bring an end to Polish anti-Semitic outrages.

Basically, Polish Jews found themselves between a rock and a hard place. They sensed disaster but fervently believed that their God would not abandon them. Besides, Hitler's threat to exterminate all Jews was not taken seriously by its intended victims. It was simply too far-fetched and impossible to comprehend.

So no one was concerned when, several days after the occupation, posters and placards began to appear on walls and kiosks all over the city, each one bringing notification of new restrictions. First, there was a curfew. Then all arms and ammunition had to be handed over. Then all radios were confiscated. All of these restrictions carried the same penalty for noncompliance. Death. But these restrictions were meant for the entire population, and we considered them routine for an occupying army.

Within days, restrictions pertaining to Jews only began to appear. Almost immediately Germans came to Jewish neighborhoods on a hunt for Jewish males, whom they forced to perform menial tasks while they beat and abused them. The Orthodox were the first to suffer. The Germans would take particular delight in tormenting these people. They cut their beards and made them eat pork in front of their children, mockingly imploring them to seek God's help.

Next came a spate of laws depriving Jews of their economic livelihood. My father had worked for an ethnic German firm which manufactured leather in a factory once owned by my paternal grandfather. My father had been in charge of procuring hides for the factory as well as for wealthy speculators. In addition to his salaried job, he would also buy leather hides for himself and speculate in the market, much as it is done now on the commodity exchanges.

The factory was located on the outskirts of the city, and my father sold the finished product from an office/warehouse in town when he was not traveling. When the Nazis occupied Radom, my father had a substantial amount of leather in the process of being finished. Just before the war started, he brought home a few packages of leather, something he had never done before.

The law that affected me the most at the time was the closing of all Jewish schools. It was not long before clandestine Jewish schools began to operate, and my parents insisted that I join one. I found myself in a group of about fifteen boys and girls, learning a normal high school curriculum in an apartment in secret. The allure of danger, the conspiratorial nature of learning, and my parents' painful economic sacrifice all led me to really apply myself to the learning process for the first time in my young life. I took part in all discussions, I did my homework diligently, and I soon noticed that Miss Soboll, the young lady who was our teacher, would call on me for answers that no one else seemed to know. I began to develop a reputation as a good student, something that was new to me. I don't remember the subject of the written assignment Miss Soboll gave us one day, but I will never forget my reaction when she read mine aloud in the class as an example of good writing.

That day, the girl who sat next to me, Ella Psherover, asked me to walk her home. She introduced me to her mother as the best writer in the class. Her mother was impressed, and Ella became my close friend.

I was overwhelmed with pride because of this scholastic ability, which I didn't know I possessed. I felt a whole new world of knowledge opening before me. I read Tolstoy, Dostoevsky, Emile Zola, Sienkiewicz, and others. I took French, English, Latin, and German—languages that helped keep me alive in the ensuing years. And all of this love of learning I discovered on the ragged edge of the approaching disaster.

I remember that once a German Wehrmacht officer stumbled into the apartment where Miss Soboll was conducting one of our classes. Even though this was early in the war and the full fury of Nazi barbarism was not yet unleashed, the penalty for an underground Jewish school was still death. He could have shot us all on the spot and been commended for it.

Fortunately, the subject of the class at the time was German. It took him a while to realize what he had come across, but as soon as he saw how frightened we were, he assured us he wouldn't harm us. It turned out he was a former professor of literature in one of the German universities. He even helped Miss Soboll conduct her class for a few minutes, then wished us well, and departed.

In November of 1939, my oldest brother Abram, twenty at the time, decided he would try to escape to the Eastern side of Poland, which had been occupied by Russia. Many people were doing that since the border was not yet well defined. I remember the night he suggested it, we all gathered around the table.

My mother's argument was basic. "Abram, stay. Whatever the future has in store for us, let's face it together."

"Yes," Bluma said. "The letters from those who are already there say that most of them want to come back. As bad as the situation is over here, it must be even worse there."

Indeed, many people were coming back. When the Russian-controlled zone of Poland swelled with hundreds of thousands of refugees streaming in from the German side, the Communists made no provisions to accommodate them. Many were arrested by the secret police, accused of being German spies, sentenced in kangaroo courts, and sent deep within Russia to the gulags. Those left behind were caught in a massive famine brought on by Russian incompetence.

Abram shook his head. "No matter how bad things are there, no one will dare call me a dirty Jew. For once in my life, I want to be able to walk in the street without being afraid of anti-Semitic hooligans."

"What good is it to walk the streets freely if you have no home to sleep in," my father said, "or if you are constantly hungry and afraid of being arrested as a spy?"

Eli pounded the table. "We must do something while we still can. The Nazis will grind us into the dust, as soon as they consolidate their victory. They'll never let us live in peace."

"It's not clear yet there is a victory," my father said. "The British and French are in the war now, and how long can Hitler last against the British navy and the mighty French army? In a few months, this war may be over."

"But Papa," Abram said, "how can I stay here in hiding like a rat most of the time? How can I let myself be humiliated daily, when I know I have a choice?"

"But these are Germans," my father said. "I can't believe that the people I remember from the Great War have suddenly turned into monsters. No, what we have here in

Radom is just a bunch of SS hoodlums who are acting without orders. How is it possible to turn a cultured people, the pillar of western morality into savages in such a short time?"

And so the arguments continued, that night and over the next several days. The decision to break up the family was quite painful, but eventually Abram's plan was approved, and the family prepared to say good-bye to the first member to leave home for good. My mother was brokenhearted, but she realized in the end that the time had come, and it was the only thing to do.

In the dead of night, defying the curfew, I accompanied Abram to a truck stop, where a vehicle was to take him to the border. A for-hire smuggling ring operated right under the noses of the Gestapo, shuttling people back and forth over the newly defined Russo-German border. Abram would write a prearranged note once he was safely across, and the smugglers would present the note to us as proof of delivery in order to receive payment.

As I walked with Abram that night, a two-man German military patrol came out of nowhere and stopped us. They trained their guns on us and ordered us to raise our hands. They asked many questions and searched Abram's backpack under a streetlight.

Among my brothers personal things, they came across a manuscript on math and physics.

One of the soldiers took a particular interest in the math and physics equations, asking Abram all kinds of questions about the notes. He turned out to be a math and physics teacher by profession and was very impressed with the manuscript. Eventually they accepted my brother's made-up explanation for breaking curfew, wished us good luck, and waved us on.

I loved my brother Abram and respected him greatly. He was tall and thin, rather pale and gaunt, and was always studying or reading books. When he was ten years old, his friends nicknamed him "Doctor." His only recreation was chess. Just like the rest of the family, I always believed that he would be a famous scientist one day.

I said good-bye to Abram that night and never saw him again.

As the winter of 1939 settled in, life under the occupation began to tighten. Before he'd left for Russia, my brother Abram was able to withdraw several hundred zlotys from his bank savings account to take with him. But in mid-November, all Jewish assets were confiscated, and my father was officially dismissed from his job. Still, my father stayed in touch with his German employers, the Burghardt brothers, a connection that helped us survive.

For the Burghardts, the war was a financial bonanza. They became the arbiters of the Jewish assets—including my father's share in their factory—and were able to make a fortune by selling confiscated Jewish-owned leather back to the Jews on the black market.

My father became their go-between in these black-market transactions, with my brother Eli and me often acting as couriers and delivery boys. My father would sell leather from the Burghardt factory to clandestine buyers for Polish zlotys or German marks and make a profit. Then since his German bosses had no faith in the value of zlotys or marks—for good reason, since the currencies soon became nearly worthless—he would exchange the money for dollars or other valuables available on the black market, and again make a profit.

He was also able to sell the several packages of leather he had brought home before the invasion "just in case," and these sales allowed us to stockpile staples like potatoes, coal, flour, cucumbers, and cabbage that we would need for the oncoming winter.

While all this sounds good, there was a tremendous risk involved as my father, my brother, and I moved black-market goods through the city. At this time, the Germans would often swoop down on Jewish neighborhoods, grab people at random, and either beat them up, insult them, or make them perform demeaning tasks such as cleaning toilets or scrubbing sidewalks. If any of us were caught with contraband, we could face anything from a heavy fine to deportation to a concentration camp to torture and execution in the Gestapo cellar.

My friend Moniek Ackerman, who also smuggled leather for his father, and I were caught several times in such dragnets, but we were always able to talk our way out by denying that we were Jews. This was before we were required to carry identity papers, and the Germans, unlike the Gentile Poles, could not recognize semitic features. In fact Jews looked more like Germans because they did not have Slavic characteristics. Also, most German officials were corrupt and bribable, and we were very careful to avoid getting caught. So for a time it was possible to get along, and the older generation, remembering the Germans of the last war, thought that things might work out after all.

It was just after the smuggling began that we received the first letter from Abram. In the letter, he confirmed the stories we had heard of the treatment that refugees from the

Germans faced under the Russians. There was famine, and thousands of people were sleeping in the streets and freezing to death. Most refugees longed to come back to their homes and families, but not my brother. He was steadfast in his distrust of the Nazis. "I will sleep in the street and use a rock for a pillow," he wrote. "I will endure hunger and other hardships, but I will never give up my newfound freedom as a man among men."

In his next letter, he told us that he was placed in a small town called Marionowka, near the city of Lootsk as a teacher in a grade school. The family was ecstatic.

It was in this atmosphere of fear and cautious optimism that my parents decided that I should have my Bar-Mitzvah. I had turned thirteen on November 15, 1939, and they asked Rabbi Chaim who lived in our complex to prepare me for the rite. After a few sessions, Rabbi Chaim pronounced me ready, and a date was set for the following Shabat.

Under the German occupation, anything that had to do with the Jewish religion was forbidden upon pain of death, so to limit exposure to danger while praying, Rabbi Chaim had sealed off a room in his apartment by blocking the door with a large wooden wardrobe. It was in this hidden room that I and a few family members and friends met for the ritual that made me a Jewish man.

While I was reciting the prayers, I heard the Germans break into the room outside in search of male workers. In the room behind the wardrobe, we all froze.

"Where's your husband?" we heard one of the Germans scream. "Where are the other Jewish pigs?"

"I don't know, sir," Rabbi Chaim's wife said. "I don't know when he'll be back, sir. Perhaps—"

"Shut up! I know they're here. I can smell them."

We listened without breathing while the Germans searched the premises thoroughly. At one point, we could hear them banging around in the wardrobe that blocked the entrance to our room, but miraculously they did not discover the door behind it.

After what seemed like an eternity, the Germans left. I looked around the room to see if I should continue praying. All around me, my family and friends nodded. I prayed that day like never before.

Soon after this incident, the order came for all Jews to wear a white armband with a blue Jewish star so they could be instantly identified. If you were caught without it, the punishment was death. Armbands had to be worn on the right arm to signify the low racial standing of Jews. The Third Reich used a plethora of armbands to identify many high-ranking party functionaries and different branches of the Hitler-Jugend, but they were all worn on the left arm.

The armband didn't stop my friend and fellow smuggler Moniek Ackerman and me. We were still permitted to own bicycles, and the two of us constantly used the bikes to smuggle leather.

In the spring of 1940, Moniek and I hatched a scheme. We knew that if we could find a way to get leather several miles beyond the city limits, we could fetch about three times the going price. In addition, we could convert the money directly into foodstuffs, which would be a great help to our families. But we also knew that if we told our parents of the plan, they would never let us do it because it was too dangerous to smuggle beyond the city limits. So Moniek arranged to rent a horse and wagon that belonged to a poor man he knew—the wagon was equipped with a double bottom built especially for the purpose of hiding black-market contraband—and both of us asked our fathers for a small amount of leather for an unnamed customer.

Early one morning, Moniek and I rode our bikes to the man's stable, picked up the horse and wagon, loaded our leather, and started out for a nearby farm village, no more than five or six miles away. As soon as we left the city limits, we took off the armbands that identified us as Jews. Those were the days before the establishment of the ghetto, but Jews were still forbidden to travel unless they obtained special permits. If we were discovered, we would have been shot on the spot even if the leather was never found. We were young and foolish and convinced that we were immortal.

At first the journey was pleasant. The day was beautiful, and the horse seemed to be responding to Moniek's direction—neither of us had much experience with horses. I was looking forward to seeing the delight on my father's face when we arrived with a wagonload of food. But when we were about halfway to our destination, I noticed that the horse seemed ever more reluctant to continue. He would buck, then stop. Each time that happened, we had a harder time getting him to move again. We both began to sweat under the sun. The whole plan—and our lives—depended on not attracting attention.

Finally the horse stopped altogether and refused to budge. We stood there in the middle of the road, not knowing what to do when two *Feld Gendarmerie* (military police) passed us on a motorcycle with a sidecar. We watched in horror as they turned around and headed back to us. We could not possibly outrun them even if there was somewhere to run to.

They stopped, and the policeman in the sidecar went straight for the horse without questioning us.

MARK IT WITH A STONE / 47

"You poor thing." He stroked the horse's neck. "These boys don't know how to treat you right!"

As soon as the horse felt the touch of the German's hand, he put his ears up and began to nuzzle the German's pockets.

The policeman turned to us. "Where is this horse's food? Don't you know it's criminal to treat a horse like this?"

I had seen an empty bag with traces of oats lying near the front seat. I grabbed it now and jumped down. As soon as the horse saw and smelled the oats, he began to prance a little.

Both Germans laughed. "You see, Kurt, it's a good thing we invaded," the other one said.

"For the horses at least."

The one who stroked the horse pointed to Moniek. "Where are you going?"

Moniek nodded down the road. "To my uncle's farm, a few kilometers ahead."

"Very well, as soon as you get there, see that you find some oats for the horse."

He then became more serious and gave us a stern lecture on how to treat animals. He walked toward the motorcycle but turned to us before he climbed in. "Get some fodder for that horse, *Donner Wetter! Schnell!*" He got back into the sidecar, and they roared off.

We made it to our destination. One of us walked backward holding out the empty bag of oats. The horse followed the smell trying to reach his familiar feeding bag.

We fed the horse as soon as we reached the farm village. We then sold our leather and loaded the wagon with fresh foods from the farms that were difficult to obtain in the city. We also made sure that we had enough oats for the return trip.

That evening we returned the horse and wagon to its owner and told him about the empty feeding bag. He was visibly embarrassed.

"I am sorry about that," he said, "but how can I feed my horse when I have no food for my wife and children?"

He was not alone. Food was becoming scarce by this time as more and more families were deprived of the opportunity to earn a living. And the worst was about to begin.

CHAPTER 3

THE LARGE GHETTO

In March 1941, the Nazis created two ghetto areas in Radom: Walowa, which held about 25,000 people, and Glinice with about 10,000. There were many reasons for the establishment of the ghettos. The first and most important was to keep the Jews concentrated in small areas for the sake of easy access. Also, ghettos were administered by Jewish councils and their auxiliaries, which freed up manpower the Nazis needed to prosecute the war. The councils and auxiliaries were made responsible with their lives for the execution of Nazi orders, which gradually became more brutal with the passage of time.

With fifty years of hindsight, I can now see the third reason for the ghettos. In the war against the Jews, the Germans needed to establish the ghettos in German-occupied Poland as a temporary holding action because the "Final Solution" had not yet crystallized. America was not yet at war with the Axis powers, and world public opinion still kept the Nazi's true genocidal intent at bay.

But after their solid victory in the Norwegian campaign, the French surrender, and the British defeat at Dunkirk, the Nazis began to believe their own propaganda about being invincible on the battlefield. Their brutality against the Jews increased with each victory until it culminated in the Final Solution. That order came when the Nazis thought they had crushed the Soviet Union. They clearly felt then that they could afford to drop all pretenses of civilized behavior and move forward on their demonic scheme to kill all the Jews and enslave others the Nazis considered to be *untermenschen*—subhuman.

We all associate important world events with a time and place. I remember sitting in a makeshift barbershop waiting to get my hair cut, reading a German account of the initial crushing defeat inflicted on the vaunted Red Army about a week after June 22, 1941. I was fifteen at the time. Our ghetto was still intact, and I remember thinking that it would not make sense for the Germans to let Jews live in relative safety while they were bleeding on the front lines.

I was right. From that day on, the noose around our necks tightened. All Communists or those belonging to leftist organizations before the war were arrested. Random raids on ghetto streets for forced labor increased in frequency and brutality. Food rations were drastically reduced, compounding the starvation rate. People were picked up off the streets by marauding Germans and disappeared, never to be heard from again.

My memory of that period revolves mainly around my father, because he was the one exposed to danger daily. He carried large sums of money to pay off his contacts outside the ghetto area and risked his life every time he brought leather home for resale.

One day, as I walked home, two uniformed *Wehrmacht* soldiers strolled by me on the street. As they passed, I wondered what regular German army soldiers were doing inside the ghetto area. I found the answer when I saw them casually unholster their guns, kneel down, take aim, and begin shooting people randomly.

There was a terrible outcry, and people began running every which way to escape the massacre. The two soldiers kept aiming and shooting like they were in a shooting gallery. I dove into a doorway, waited until the shooting stopped, and ran to check the dead and wounded to see if my father was among them. I then ran home as fast as I could to make sure that my father had made it there safely. When I saw him, I threw my arms around him and cried.

Writing this does not capture the sheer terror of the event. There are times even today when I do not feel safe walking on the street. The two soldiers returned to the ghetto from time to time, and left their harvest of dead bodies on the street each time they came.

Another sign that the Nazis were tightening the noose is the story of my friend Nathan. Nathan was a beautiful boy, with black flashing eyes, straight white teeth, jet black hair, and a turned-up nose. He was the eldest son of our neighbors, Isaac and Leah. Isaac was a kosher butcher by trade, and after the Nazis created the ghettos, one of their first edicts was to summon all butchers to the Gestapo. The Nazis thought the butchers were a potential threat because they were physically strong and more likely to defy authority.

Most of the city's butchers turned themselves in, but our neighbor Isaac decided to go into hiding. It was good that he did, because as time passed, nothing was heard from the butchers who had reported to the Gestapo. The Nazis soon began an intense search for those who remained in hiding.

With his father gone, my friend Nathan, at thirteen, took over the responsibility for providing for his family. His demeanor became that of an adult—alert, swift, and agile. Every day Nathan snuck out of the ghetto area, smuggled in live animals, slaughtered them, and sold the meat to those who could afford it. In the eyes of the Nazi authorities, every step of his operation was punishable by death.

Like nearly everyone in our neighborhood, I admired Nathan tremendously. He was a true Jewish ghetto hero who defied the Nazis daily. He and I found fewer chances to spend time together, but whenever we did, our friendship blossomed. On several occasions, he even let me help him in his exploits. We had a common enemy in the Gestapo and a common goal in survival. Together, we dreamed of freedom, of the day we could escape this hateful God-forsaken country.

The Jewish ghetto administrators were increasingly pressured to deliver those on the wanted list, including Nathan's father, or face the consequences. And the consequences were becoming clearer. The Gestapo visited the ghetto frequently at night and plucked people from their beds. The administrators were eventually told to pick up their tortured bodies at Gestapo headquarters.

Slowly we began getting used to the idea that life was cheap, particularly Jewish life.

One night I was awakened by loud noises in the building.

Half asleep, I heard German being spoken downstairs. Soon I heard heavy footsteps coming up the stairway and realized that we were about to be visited by the dreaded Gestapo. With each of their steps closer to our door, my heart beat faster. Who did they want? My father? My brother Eli? Me?

But they passed our door and continued down the corridor. We heard harsh, loud commands in German to open the door. In a few minutes, it was all over.

They had taken Nathan.

At thirteen, he was their youngest victim up until that time. Somehow the community could not bring itself to believe that even the Gestapo could harm a mere child. To bolster his mother's spirit, she was told by the Jewish auxiliaries that surely the Gestapo would only interrogate Nathan about his father's whereabouts and release him. Several days passed with no word of Nathan. The ghetto was rife with terrible rumors. Everyone felt threatened. On the fourth night after Nathan's arrest, we were again awakened by steps in the corridor in the middle of the night. This time it was Leah, Nathan's mother. When my mother opened the door, Leah fell into her arms crying hysterically in a total state of shock.

When we managed to calm her, she told us she had seen it in a dream. Many bodies of men in a semicircle. They were all shot, and she knew that Nathan was one of them. She said she saw Nathan run and call, "Mama, Mama!" and fall to the ground as the bullets reached him.

We tried to tell her that it was only a dream and that there was no reason for her to believe that it actually happened, but it was to no avail. She was convinced that she had seen her son's murder in her dream. Finally, despite the curfew, I got dressed and went down to the nearby Jewish ghetto auxiliary offices to see what I could learn.

I found the people in charge highly agitated. Someone said they were awaiting bad news. At about five a.m., the telephone rang. The officer in charge picked up the receiver, and everyone present grouped around him. As he listened, his face became as white as a ghost, and he kept repeating, *"Yawohl. Yawohl."* When the conversation was over and he replaced the receiver, I could sense that something was terribly wrong.

"The Gestapo has ordered that a few covered wagons be immediately dispatched to the meadow," he said. "There are over one hundred bodies."

Within the hour, a convoy of three covered wagons was on its way. The wagons had to be covered so as not to expose its cargo to the general public outside the ghetto. I was allowed to go along to help the doctor in case there were wounded among the bodies.

After what seemed like an eternity, the convoy came to a stop on a street that had houses on only one side. Across from the houses was a large meadow, overgrown with weeds, scattered spring flowers, and clumps of bushes. We did not have to walk far to find what we came for.

There were many times when I was to witness much more devastating scenes. But none ever made greater an impression on me than the scene in that meadow.

Men of all ages were lying in a semicircle, their hands tied behind their backs, their feet pointing inward. They were motionless and dead. One could easily imagine their executioners standing in the middle of the semicircle and spraying death with their machine guns as they pivoted.

At one point in the circle, there was a gap. Someone lying there had gotten up and made a run for it. Trancelike I walked over to the nearest bushes, the most likely place to run to. I half-expected what I found. Eyes wide open, with the eternal puzzled look, was my friend, Nathan.

His mother had been right. The instinct of the doomed told her that her son was no more. I fell upon Nathan's body, and my stream of tears mixed with the pool of his blood.

All the bodies including Nathan's were brought back to the ghetto. Nathan's father Isaac disregarded all warnings and attended funeral services for his son. When the services were over, two SS men appeared, took Isaac under each arm, and half-carried him to a waiting car across the street. They motioned for him to get in the backseat, but Isaac stood fast. One of them took the pistol from his holster and again ordered Isaac to get in the car. Again he refused, pointing to the ground. He unmistakably wanted to be shot on the spot.

The German quickly obliged.

His wife Leah went into shock and was put in an insane asylum. The remaining children were taken to the orphanage. A few months later, they were all deported to Treblinka and consumed by the flames of the Holocaust.

Historians generally regard the year 1942 to be the lowest point in the Allied effort to defeat Hitler. For the first nine months of the year, the Nazis recorded solid victories on all fronts, from Tobruk to Sevastopol. The German and Japanese forces seemed invincible in the air, on the sea, and on the ground. These successes had disastrous consequences for those under the heel of the Axis occupation. Fence-sitters in the occupied countries who had doubted the Nazis would win the ultimate victory began to embrace them and do their bidding. Then America's entry into the war against the Axis powers removed all remaining political restraints.

The infamous Wannsee Conference took place at the beginning of 1942. As the preserved minutes of this conference show, the fate of the Jews was sealed there. Those in attendance were the SS leaders chosen by Himmler to execute the Fuhrer's order for "The Final Solution of the Jewish Problem."

By this time, Jews all over Poland had been herded into ghettos, self-administered holding pens for the victims. Wherever possible the killing methods and facilities were to be kept secret. Hitler, always the consummate politician, was surprised by the German public's vehement opposition to his euthanasia killings of Germans. This opposition forced Hitler to abandon the euthanasia program in 1941. He did not want a similar protest among his own people on account of the Jews, so the largest systematic genocide in mankind's history took place under the guise of code words such as "resettlement," "aktions," and "deportation." The ghetto Theresienstadt was created in Czechoslovakia to serve as a kind of Potemkin Village. Influential German Jews who had German friends or relatives were sent to Theresienstadt, where they were held in reasonably decent conditions and allowed to write their friends and relatives in Germany. Eventually they were shipped to Auschwitz for extermination.

In the "General Government," (the Polish-occupied territories during the Second World War), the mass deportations of Jews began with the city of Lublin in March 1942. Thereafter it was only a question of logistics and the ability of the extermination factories to keep up with production.

The turn for Radom and its 35,000 Jewish inhabitants came on the night of August 5, 1942.

Until that spring, our household held up fairly well. We did not have to move because we lived in the area assigned to the ghetto, although one of my uncles and his family of six moved in and shared our living space. And my father was able to stay in touch with his former employers and friends, the Burghardts.

For some time into the war, the Burghardts were convinced that the Hitler phenomenon was an aberration that would not last. To preserve their standing in the town's business community, they were willing to help their former Jewish business associates. But when the German armies defeated the French and took Paris, their attitude changed. They reduced and eventually cut off their contact with my father and with the others as well. They may also have been informed by their high-ranking Nazi friends as to the ultimate fate in store for the Jews. In any case, my family began to see truly hard times.

Then in the summer of 1942, we began to hear rumors of deportations of entire ghetto populations. Like people stricken with a terminal disease, many in the community adopted an attitude of denial, ignoring the bad news and despising its bearers. Yet, the rumors persisted.

Faced with inevitable starvation or deportation, my brother Eli and I volunteered to work in the munitions factory. The Polish workers were being phased out and sent to work in plants in Germany. Jews were being actively sought to replace them. I was chosen to work a twelve-hour night shift on the handgun production line. Eli was given a daytime shift on the rifle assembly line. Naively, we believed the German promises that our families would be protected from deportation because of our jobs.

So each day at six p.m., I reported to one of the ghetto gates, where black-uniformed Ukrainian factory guards marched us through back streets and fields of undeveloped land to the opposite side of town, where the factory was located. After six a.m. when the new shift took over, the guards marched us back to the gates of the ghetto. I was a quick enough learner and adapted easily, but the twelve-hour shifts were exhausting and extremely hard on my young body. When I came home after the night shift, I would collapse with fatigue. But as long as there was a home to come back to after work, I was glad to do it, especially if it was going to keep the family intact. On the night of August 6, 1942, we broke for lunch as usual at midnight. The heat and humidity were unbearable, and all the windows in the factory were wide open. As soon as the machinery stopped, we could hear a strange noise interspersed with volleys of automatic gunfire coming from the ghetto area. The din and the gunfire continued throughout the night.

In the morning, when it was time to line up for the march back to the ghetto, the leader of the factory guards tried frantically to call ahead for instructions. After some time elapsed, he was ordered to take us back as usual.

As soon as we entered the field that led us back to the ghetto, we came face to face with columns of deportees being marched from the ghetto to the railway station that was near the munitions factory. As soon as we saw them, our guards became agitated. There were only four of them and one hundred of us. They unslung their rifles, pointed them at us, and ordered us to trot with our heads down. But we were so close to the columns of deportees that we could not help but see their faces. I watched the SS guards who walked beside the columns in a crouch. They were so young, not much older than me. So blond, so fresh faced. They were in combat uniform, with backpacks, their submachine guns unslung, muzzles pointed at the victims, helmets tightly strapped under the chins, as if in actual combat. There were so many of them. They seemed entranced and determined, as if they were on a holy mission. They were clearly elite troops, on special assignment.

I remember thinking of Becker, a very nice ethnic German boy I befriended long ago in Pionki. In the early days of the occupation, he would take me and Moniek to the movies. He would protect us in his imposing black uniform. Could he be among them?

As we got further into the field, a panorama of sheer hell unfolded. Abandoned baby carriages were all over the place. Some held dead babies with their dead mothers lying beside them grotesquely in the early morning sun. There were corpses all over, some clutching the dead infants, others holding a bundle or a suitcase in a deadly grip. One elderly woman was sitting atop her suitcase screaming and berating God. She had been shot through the chest, and where she sat, there was a large pool of blood.

Barking German shepherds were straining at their leashes to get at the victims, guns were fired constantly, and people were toppling over silently like marionettes. *Schnell, Schnell*. German curses reverberated in the morning air, and all the time the columns of humanity kept moving towards the railroad siding and oblivion.

I kept darting glances at the sky. I half-expected some miracle to happen. But the early morning sun looked on unblinking, and the wildflowers smelled as sweetly as on any other summer day. Nature observed, completely oblivious, and I knew it was hopeless.

Then it happened. One of the boys from our column recognized his parents. In a split second, he bolted from our ranks, ran over, and embraced them. The commotion he created was too much for the SS to overlook. They stopped the column, pulled out the parents with their son, and shot them.

After that several others saw relatives, sisters, brothers, or parents, but there were no more outcries. The only sign they had recognized someone among the deportees was the grief and despair in their faces.

We continued trotting until we reached the ghetto gates. Our guards informed the officer in charge of our status as munitions factory workers. Our group was allowed to enter the ghetto and stand in a yard until further notice.

A short time later, a staff car full of SS arrived and announced the end of the *aktion*. All the available freight cars had been filled. Our guards were told to leave the ghetto. We were admonished to report for work in the evening as usual or face the consequences. Then we were set free to go home.

I started walking cautiously toward the house. SS were still all over the ghetto area. Their job for the day was done, and they chatted amiably about the experience. I passed the central market street where a large crowd was still gathered. That was where the selection took place. Only minutes before, a German finger would point to life or death. Now the Germans were gone. I began to run toward the house.

It was not even eight a.m., but for me the day was longer than a lifetime. And the longest part was the several minutes it took to sprint across the ghetto to our house. I prayed as I ran through the deserted streets. I took shortcuts, hopped over fences, ran through a back field, and finally got to the back of the house.

Standing there in the morning mist, facing east, was little Rabbi Chaim, who had risked his life to officiate at my Bar-Mitzvah. He was wrapped in his Talit, and he was praying as I had never heard anyone pray. When he saw me, he stopped. I looked at his face, and he looked at mine, and we saw the agony of our people reflected in each other. We embraced and we cried.

I told him what I knew, that the Germans had liquidated the smaller ghetto of Glinice during the night and, when they found more room on the freight cars, came in the early hours of the morning to our ghetto, Walowa, to finish the job. I told him that it was over for now, and the Germans were gone. Then I went upstairs to see my family.

I knew that my parents and my sister were still safe, at least for the time being. I also knew that my brother Eli was back at the munitions factory. Because of his work schedule, he would have left for work before the *aktion* in our ghetto started.

Even now, as I write this more than fifty years later, I can still feel the relief I felt that day. And it was so foolish. More than ten thousand people were taken that day, and more would have been taken if there were more cattle cars. Only a short reprieve was given to the rest of us, and only because of logistics.

I climbed the two flights of stairs to our apartment as I always did, two at the time. The building was strangely silent—I did not even hear the usual noise of children—and all doors were closed. I drank in every stair, every door, the hallways, the windows that looked out into the courtyard, all this great playground of my childhood. I absorbed it all deeply.

Then I opened our door and fell upon my father. I loved him more than ever before. Then I embraced my mother and my sister, Bluma. They were all dressed for a journey. Two suitcases and a backpack were near the door. In spite of all that we knew, we still clung desperately to the hope that "deportation" was nothing more than a change of address. The denial syndrome was still there.

I told them what I knew, that they were safe for the time being. They relaxed and began to ask questions. I washed up, and my mother brought me something to eat. While I ate, I looked at my father and my heart sank.

He looked so old, at fifty-two, so broken. He seemed embarrassed for having failed to provide his family with the necessary survival tools. A giant of a man reduced to impotence by cruel forces he could not control, he had come to depend on the goodwill of the hated Germans to save the family, and now that goodwill was at an end. He told me that shortly after my brother Eli had left the house before five a.m. shooting began on the opposite side of the ghetto. His worst fears were about to come true. Everyone huddled indoors, with all their worldly possessions stuffed in bags, waiting for the inevitable German shriek of *ALLE JUDEN RAUS*. I was the first to come with the news that the German monster had devoured his fill for that day.

My father then went outside to notify the neighbors of the news I brought. As if by magic, the familiar noises returned. Doors and windows opened, and people went back to the business of living.

My mother made me go to bed. She told me I had to rest after this terrible ordeal and get ready for work again. I went to bed, but sleep eluded me. I had not told my parents of what I saw in the field that day, but I could not stop thinking about it. I remember thinking in my adolescent innocence that if I could just talk to Hitler and explain how terribly people were suffering because of his policies, he would listen and bring a stop to it. I could not imagine that the Germans, an enlightened, cultured, and educated people could make the cold-blooded murder of men, women, and children state policy.

I was also kept awake by visions of my dear friends whom I cherished. I saw Ella, her beautiful sparkling eyes greeting me with gladness every time she saw me. I saw her mother looking on with approval whenever she saw us together. I loved her mother's comment that Ella and I made a lovely couple. This was my first stirring of love and romance, so beautiful and promising, yet so impossible. Finally, my head filled with my dreams, my family, my people, and above all, my feeling of total impotence and hopelessness, I dozed. When I finally woke, my head was spinning, and I had trouble focusing.

When I got out of bed, I saw my mother packing some of my things into a bag. "Mama, what are you doing?" I asked.

"This is for you to take along to work in case they don't let you return to the ghetto."

I grabbed her hands. "No, wait, Mama, I am not going back to work. Whatever happens, we should stay together."

"Don't be ridiculous, you have to go. Now go and get washed."

As on so many previous occasions, the vehemence of her answer precluded any further discussion.

My mother finished packing my bag and prepared a plate of my favorite soup. She put some of the soup into a container that was part of an imported tea set, a treasured kitchen ornament. These containers had pictures of faraway exotic places on them, and they were always a part of my travel dreams. She put the container carefully in my bag so it would not spill.

When I finished eating, it was time to go.

I first approached Bluma to say good-bye. She had tears streaming down her face.

Bluma was so attached to my mother that she would not hear of going to work to obtain an exemption from deportation. She had made it crystal clear from the time the rumors started that she would stay with my mother and father no matter what. She was nineteen years old. I was actually glad Bluma was with my parents. It helps ease the guilt pangs I still suffer to this day for having, in effect, abandoned them myself.

Bluma handed me two gold coins that had been camouflaged as covered buttons on a sweater she wore. I knew that these coins were the family's only remaining valuables, and I refused to take them.

I kissed Bluma's tear-stained face and turned toward my mother. For the first time in my life, I saw my mother's face without her stern composure. She gathered me in her arms and for the first time ever told me how much she loved me and how proud she was of me. She told me to live by the values she had taught me. She put her hands over my head, blessed me, and wished me Godspeed.

The hardest of all was to say good-bye to my father. To this day I think that watching my father disintegrate and suffer affected me more than any other experience. I just could not bear to see him helpless. I embraced him silently, we looked at each other knowing full well that it was the last time. Then he patted me gently on the head, as he had so many times before. He tried to speak, but all that came out was a violent sob.

I grabbed my bag, turned on my heels, and left my home.

As my mother had foreseen, when it was time for us to go home that day after work, orders came to quarter us on the factory premises. Eli's unit was held back as well.

Neither of us ever saw our loved ones again.

Two weeks later on August 15, 1942, extra lights and reflectors were installed in the ghetto. I heard later that special *Einsatz* units arrived and circled the ghetto. Anyone attempting to leave the area was shot without questions.

All we heard at the munitions factory were bursts of gunfire night and day. During that time, I was in a mental vacuum. I could not think, I could not eat, my mouth was constantly dry. My work became slipshod, and the foreman warned me that I made too many rejects. Other boys covered for me, but rejects meant sabotage, and sabotage was certain death.

When my brother Eli and I saw each other occasionally—steady contact was impossible because of our work schedule—he implored me not to break down. He said that perhaps our loved ones had only been sent to the Ukraine to till the land, a common canard devised to rationalize our continued existence in slavery. I did not believe it, but at the same time it was even harder to believe the truth. What on earth could they do with so many people?

After three days, the gunfire stopped, and there was an eerie silence. We workers continued to be quartered at the factory.

For weeks I lived in mental agony. I avoided anyone who knew me and stopped caring for my appearance. Life was not worth living, and I started to think of the easiest way to end it.

Then a miracle. Someone brought me a letter with some money from Moniek Ackerman. He and his entire family had survived the mass roundups intact by hiding during the deportation and, after it was over, returning to the one small ghetto the Germans still maintained. Moniek had heard of my predicament and sent the letter with the money through a Jewish orderly whose job was to be the liaison between the different Jewish work camps. In the letter, Moniek offered me a place to stay and any help I would need if I could escape from the munitions factory to the small ghetto. Moniek's letter meant hope, destiny, and the love and support of people who cared.

All at once, there was a spring in my step. I bought food and soap with some of the money and began to take care of myself. I now had something to live for. Escape.

I also began feeling angry instead of sorry, and for the first time, I thought the sweetest thought of all. Maybe, just maybe, if I could survive, there was a chance at revenge. A chance to see the super-German defeated and true justice meted out.

For the next several weeks, I recovered my strength. I shared some of Moniek's money with my brother Eli and told him of my plan to escape. He encouraged me to do it. I noticed that with this new determination my entire body became alert, more resilient and more determined, as if nature cooperated with me in the task of survival. And more and more, I kept thinking of the sweet scent of revenge.

For several weeks after the liquidation of the large ghettos, all workers at the munitions factory were quartered on factory premises in conditions that were abysmal even by Nazi standards. Presently a concentration camp surrounded with barbed wire was built on nearby Szkolna Street to accommodate us. My work unit was one of the first to be transferred to the new campsite.

Our guards established a new routine. We were lined up twice daily for a roll call after which different units formed according to their job assignments. Each unit then marched, under guard, to and from the munitions factory, two miles from the camp.

I began to plot my escape in a surprisingly lucid, coherent manner. It was too dangerous to share my plan with anyone—escapes were punished by collective retribution—but in my mind, I kept careful track of the timing of all activities. Winter was approaching, and it was getting darker each day as we marched to meet the six p.m. start-up time. Each time we marched, I noted more and more opportunities to slip away, without being noticed immediately. I made sure that I walked with someone different each day so I would not be missed by a companion, or expose anyone to special punishment for being a friend of the escapee.

But before I could find the right opportunity, I ran out of the money Moniek sent me. I was always hungry, and my body started deteriorating again. I also developed a violent cough that caused me severe pain. I knew that I had to act soon because once malnutrition set in, I would lose the will to fight. Next would come the indifference to my surroundings, vacant eyes, swelling at the ankles, and the slow descent into oblivion. I had seen the pattern thousands of times in the ghetto and was seeing it again in people around me.

I was much too proud to ask for help from those who still had the means to augment the meager rations we received for our work. My father's brother, Maylech, and his three sons were also munitions factory workers, and one of the boys was an orderly, which gave their family an advantage. I would sometimes watch them from afar when they were eating, but I never made an attempt to contact them.

By November of 1942, the harsh Polish winter was almost upon us, and I decided it was time. My brother Eli's unit still had not been transferred to the new camp, and I didn't have a chance to see him at the factory. Finally I wrote him a note and asked a friend to deliver it when he saw him. In the note I apprised him of my plan, bid him good-bye, and reminded him of our family pledge to meet in Palestine one day, if any of us survived.

The following day, I put on as many layers of clothing as I could, stuffed my pockets with the few personal belongings I still possessed, and took a place in the middle of the column at the extreme right for the march to the factory.

I knew the exact spot where I was going to make the break. The streets were dark—the streetlights were quite dim—but it was still early enough that there were "free" people walking on the sidewalks. When the column rounded a corner, I simply took a few steps to the side and joined some pedestrians in an unhurried gait.

I walked normally for a few minutes though my heart was pounding so loudly I was afraid people might hear it. As soon as another corner came up, I turned in the general direction of the small ghetto on the opposite side of town.

The curfew wasn't on until nine o'clock. That gave me ample time to cover the few miles to the ghetto. All I needed was enough luck not to be stopped for an I.D. check. I stuck my hand in my pocket and took out a cigarette, one of four I had bought with the last of Moniek's money.

The brand name of the cigarettes was "Yunak." They came in a long paper filter with only about two inches stuffed with tobacco. I'd had considerable doubts about the wisdom of investing my only resources in the purchase of tobacco, which we knew was deadly even then, especially for the undernourished. But I made my decision for medicinal reasons—I knew I would need something to calm me.

I went to light the cigarette and realized I did not have matches.

I held the cigarette in my hand while I walked and thought of asking someone for a light, but the risk of it always stopped me. I was afraid my Jewish features might show in the matchlight, or my hands would tremble and give me away. So I continued to walk briskly, with the unlighted cigarette in my hand.

After a few blocks, I decided to take a shortcut through some back streets that I thought were probably safer. It wasn't long before I came into a street that was completely dark. On one side of it was a tall fence topped with barbed wire. Behind that fence were warehouses that belonged to the munitions factory. I walked on the opposite side of the street in pitch-black darkness and felt elated. I hated the dreadful munitions factory, and it felt good just to be walking freely on the other side of the fence.

My eyes adjusted to the darkness, and I could make out contours of buildings in the distance. Then out of the darkness came a sharp command. *"Halt, Steinbleiben!"*

I froze immediately and raised my hands above my head. A flashlight beam passed over my face then slowly moved down the rest of my body. I heard someone walking towards me.

"Ausweis! Papieren!"

I could now make out the outline of a helmet and a rifle slung over the right shoulder. I stuck my hand in the left breast pocket of my jacket and slowly took out my wallet, which was stuffed with pictures of my family and other papers in addition to my identity documents. Unfortunately, the documents were all stamped with the most condemnatory word of that time, *Jude*.

I was calm and controlled, but I made believe that I was so frightened that I couldn't find the right identity paper. I pulled out several, held them in the beam of the flashlight, which he held directly over me, and put them back with seeming annoyance. I knew I'd have to make a run for it and was buying time until the right moment came.

Suddenly we heard the unmistakable click of heeled shoes on the opposite side of the street. The beam of the flashlight swung away from me, and instantly I folded my wallet and started running in a zigzag.

Behind me came an outraged *"Steinbleiben,"* then several shots. The bullets whizzed by me, but I was moving as fast as my young legs and adrenaline would take me.

I ran perhaps two miles before I felt it was safe to stop. Then I turned away from the ghetto—they might set up a dragnet if they thought a Jew was involved. Presently I found a multifamily house with a stairway to an unoccupied basement. I hid behind the stairway and tried to relax.

I was in shambles. I felt less worthy than an animal. A stray dog could walk the streets unmolested, but the whole might of the Third Reich would be enlisted to hunt down me or any other Jew who didn't cooperate in our own destruction. I began to realize that we are all destined to die. The lucky ones were the ones who went sooner with less pain.

I stayed in the cellar for a while, it was warm and comfortable. But I knew I faced certain death if I were discovered in the morning. Eventually I went out into the street again, this time determined to get my cigarette lit. I badly needed to calm myself.

I stopped the first person I saw smoking and motioned to him that I needed a light. He hesitated for a moment because the street was almost deserted, but then he extended his cigarette. I carefully puffed on my own so as not to damage his, and the glow of the two cigarettes revealed the contour of my face. My hands were shaking.

I thanked him for his kindness.

"Go with God," he said. I was sure he knew I was a Jew on the run.

I kept walking toward the ghetto. I had heard that the small ghetto was only two city blocks closed off with fences and walls with guards at the entry gate and patrolling the whole perimeter on the outside. The closer I got, the more dangerous it was. Finally at around midnight, I arrived at an abandoned building where I could observe a part of the ghetto wall. I waited.

Soon two gendarmes came by on bicycles armed with hand machine guns. They swept the perimeter slowly. Within a few minutes, another patrol arrived, then another. I waited and watched the patrols for quite a while until I was sure of the timing.

I decided to make a dry run first to reconnoiter the point of entry. As soon as the last patrol was out of sight, I ran across the wide, brightly lit street to a gate that was part of a wall, the most likely place to make it over. I looked up at the gate and began to climb. It proved fairly easy, and I decided to go all the way, but then I slipped and fell back.

I glanced each way, began to climb again, vaulted over the top, and dropped down on the other side just as the next patrol rounded the curb outside. I lay motionless and watched them go by.

Once inside the ghetto, I realized that I knew many people there besides Moniek, but I didn't know where anyone lived. Then I thought of Ella. Her family had lived in this two-block area before the deportations, and it was possible they still lived in the same place. I walked to the building, climbed the familiar two flights of stairs, and knocked on the door.

A frightened voice asked who was there. It was Ella's mother.

I identified myself quietly so as not to disturb the neighbors. From inside the apartment, I heard a commotion and the door opened.

For a long moment, Ella, her mother, and her sister just stared at me as if I had returned from another world. Then they threw their arms around me and drew me inside. Ella's mother started preparing something to eat.

I took in the scene of a home I knew so well and missed so much. I was overwhelmed with their kindness. Slowly I began to realize that I had returned from another world. I had come back from the dead, at least temporarily. As the realization set in, I felt my feet going numb under me, and the room began to spin.

For the first time ever, I fell into a dead faint.

CHAPTER 4

SMALL GHETTO, THIRD DEPORTATION

When I awoke in Ella's apartment, I had trouble focusing. I knew I was safe for the moment, but the fear of the hunted was still with me.

Ella was the first to notice that I was up. She came over and placed a moist cloth gently on my forehead. Her eyes were enormous and most beautiful.

I was somewhat embarrassed for having barged in on them. I did not feel close enough to ask her and her family to shelter a fugitive. I apologized for intruding.

She didn't answer but instead told me about her family. Her sister Celina had already left for work, her mother was still asleep. Her father, Mr. Psherover, had been a ghetto orderly. Some months earlier he had been arrested by the Gestapo, and they had not heard from him since.

I asked Ella about all our friends from Miss Soboll's class. We had kept close in spite of the terror of life in the ghetto. Miss Soboll imbued us with a special kind of loyalty toward each other and helped us maintain our decency in spite of the ghastly surroundings.

Ella gave me a rundown of those who survived the deportations and were either in the small ghetto or quartered in factories producing goods for the war effort. I told her about the help Moniek offered me, and she told me that Moniek's entire family had survived due to a close friendship his father had developed with a high-ranking SS officer. She also said that Moniek talked about me constantly and that he was awaiting my arrival. I took heart on hearing this and wanted to go to Moniek's apartment immediately, but Ella held me back.

"Let's wait till it gets dark," she said. "It'll be much safer then. Now you might be recognized by an orderly who knows you. And if you are caught as a fugitive, they'll send you back to the munitions factory for punishment."

I nodded. We both knew what that meant.

By this time, Mrs. Psherover was out of bed and getting dressed. People had gotten used to living in cramped quarters that afforded little privacy. Women especially became adept at getting in and out of clothing without embarrassment even if they had to dress or undress in front of men.

When she finished dressing and washing, Mrs. Psherover turned towards me. "You gave us a real scare last night, but

I'm glad you came to Ella and us. You already look a lot better. Just give me a chance, and I'll put up a pot of tea."

Ella helped her mother prepare breakfast, which consisted of tea with bread and marmalade.

"We heard terrible things about the treatment of Jewish workers in the Daimler factory," Ella said as they bustled about.

"They're all true," I said.

"Please tell us about it."

I started talking about the harsh treatment we suffered at the hands of our Austrian masters, the civilian corporate engineers who took over responsibility for production. I told them of the twelve-hour shifts and the brutal beatings for the smallest infraction of the rules. I told them of one Austrian engineer named Miller who was in charge of a section of young Jewish women and how he would pick a different girl each night to sexually abuse. Mrs. Psherover and Ella listened to my tales of horror, and tears welled up in their eyes.

"This is a terrible time to be a parent," Mrs. Psherover said. "When you can't protect your child from such depravities, perhaps it is best to put an end to it."

"But some of us must live and carry on," Ella said. "No matter what, I can't believe that the world is aware of what's going on here and remains silent."

I spent the day with Ella and her mother. In the evening when it was time to go, I embraced Mrs. Psherover and told her that I would never forget her kindness. Ella walked with me to a two-story building on the next street. We climbed one flight of stairs, and Ella knocked gently on a door.

The door opened, and there were the blue-gray eyes, tousled hair, and genial, happy face of my dearest friend,

Moniek. We embraced in total silence. What was there to say? Our friendship, loyalty and love for each other had been strengthened by years of living in the shadow of death. We were two boys in complete harmony with each other, inseparable, together no matter what.

Moniek's family welcomed me, and as they were about to eat dinner, they invited Ella and me to join them. Ella declined, curtsied smartly, and bid all good-bye. She told me that we would see each other soon.

I sat that evening at the Ackerman family table, and I could not believe my good fortune. There were foods there that I had forgotten existed. There was chicken soup with rice and lima beans—an old favorite of mine—chicken and boiled beef. Luxury foods that only the very rich could still afford. I tried to eat sparingly so as not to seem beggarly, but it was not easy.

When the meal was finished, Moniek took me up to the attic. Flashlight in hand he showed me the sleeping quarters he had prepared for me. In a far corner, invisible from the entrance, there was a sofa, a table and chair—palatial accommodations after where I had been. On the table was an oil lamp which he lit, then we sat down and talked until very late.

This corner of the Ackerman attic was to be my home for the duration. Moniek assured me that this building would be safest for me because influential people lived there, and the ghetto orderlies would not dare search it. I would hide out here by day until Moniek's contacts could legitimize my stay in the ghetto and get me a food-ration card. At night it would be possible for me to go out, providing I saw only a few of our friends who could be trusted.

A new phase of my destiny was unfolding. I was alone now and totally dependent on the goodwill and generosity of friends.

The following morning, Moniek came up with another friend, Lustig, who lived with his parents in the same building. I remembered him from before. He was a good ice skater, and we had a lot of fun skating together in bygone days. That evening the three of us ventured out into the street for the first time. We met some friends, boys and girls, but socializing in the street was forbidden, so after some discussion, we were invited to an apartment of one of the girls.

Her name was Danka Lastman. I had known her for some time when we lived in the large ghetto but never thought of her as a friend because she was only a thirteen year old among fifteen year olds. Mostly I remembered seeing her walking in the streets with a beautiful Dalmatian dog. The dog, named Till was owned by a German Abwehr (army intelligence) officer named Schultz who was quartered with the Lastman family for a considerable length of time before the formation of the ghetto. Danka became Till's guardian while Herr Schultz was at work. She loved the dog, and she would occasionally have him do his tricks when friends asked her to. I once struck up a conversation with her and found she was the youngest of five sisters, each more beautiful than the other. She also had one brother, who just before the war started had returned from Paris, where he had been studying medicine in the Sorbonne.

Now little Danka Lastman was a well-developed and extremely attractive, young woman. An angelic smile revealed two rows of straight, beautiful teeth and a pair of dimples that gave her a look of openness, sincerity, and a lust for life. Her deep-set hazel eyes were framed by slightly curled chestnut-brown hair. She was about five feet four inches and still growing, buxom and lovely to behold.

Danka told me that her family had also survived intact. Her oldest sister Lola was married to an influential orderly who was able to shelter the family from deportation.

Danka and Moniek, Ella and I, Lustig, and a few others gathered almost every evening at Danka's married sister's apartment for hushed and serious conversations. I inquired about Aamek Birenbaum who was another of Miss Soboll's students and a good friend. To my delight, Danka told me that he survived with his mother and younger brother, Davidek. Their father Motek was on the Russian side. They were quartered and working in a Wehrmacht quartermaster depot (A.V.L.), where Jewish workers were still treated decently. Mostly we talked about the atrocities that were being committed daily and the latest war news. The smallest hints of a German defeat would set our hopes soaring. We became close-knit and very aware of the precariousness of our existence. We were young, but we were already hardened by two years of everyday horror of ghetto life.

We knew we all lived in a kind of suspension between life and death. It was well known that the main reason the Germans kept the small ghetto in operation was a labor detail of several hundred workers charged with gathering, sorting, and shipping the booty of the twenty-some thousand people who had been deported. With Germans directing, the Jewish workers went block by block, street by street, house by house, taking every worthwhile item. They sorted, crated, and shipped the plundered goods to specific destinations in Germany. Ghetto inhabitants were also used as slave labor in former Jewish-owned factories that produced goods for the war effort.

It was at that time that I accidentally bumped into my uncle Hershel, my father's eldest brother, while walking in the street. I didn't know that he had survived the deportation, and when I saw him, I fell upon him crying uncontrollably. He took me to a dilapidated room where he was staying with others and gave me a piece of bread sprinkled with sugar.

"Eat, Yossek eat," he said.

While I ate, I studied him. For as long as I could remember, Uncle Hershel was a most imposing presence. He was tall and heavy-set with an unmistakable appearance of a successful burgher. He was a soft touch for some sweets, which he always had in his pocket, or sometimes even a quarter for the movies.

Now, I could hardly bear to look at him. His cheekbones were sunken, and the suit he wore was dirty and crumpled. His eyes were bloodshot. He was incoherent as to the whereabouts of his family—I think he still believed the canard about tilling the land in the Ukraine. I left him feeling terrible but somewhat relieved that my father never came down this far.

I also met my Uncle Aron-Meyer, in the small ghetto and found him in the same state. That meeting was even more emotional because our families had been extremely close. I felt I was greeting someone who had come back from the other world. Uncle Aron-Meyer told me his entire family, including their first two-year-old grandchild, had been deported. Like Uncle Hershel, he still would not admit to the bitter truth.

Both my uncles were paragons of strength and decency, role models I admired and respected. Before the war, they were well-to-do businessmen, respected in the community for their charitable contributions and business skills. When I saw them in the small ghetto, they were completely shocked and demoralized, barely hanging on to life. Being elderly (in their early fifties) and not being craftsmen, they were without meaningful survival tools. Seeing them thus stripped of their self-worth and dignity depressed me terribly.

They were both taken to Szydlowiec, a small suburb near Radom, on the third of December 1942, in an SS selection of ghetto "undesirables." Most of the people selected for Szydlowiec were never heard from again.

The SS still protected the Jewish master tailors, furriers, shoemakers, and other craftsmen. It was quite common to see high-ranking SS officers come to the small ghetto to have fancy leather coats, hats, boots, shirts, and sweaters made to order and shipped to Germany. The officers' vanity allowed a number of these fashion craftsman to survive the war, and the craftsmen had made a conscious effort to remember the home addresses in Germany where the goods were shipped. Many of these SS murderers were subsequently arrested and tried for heinous crimes after their home addresses were turned over by survivors to Allied intelligence officers.

In and among these other groups was the influx of "illegitimate" Jews who had been living as Aryans and could no longer sustain themselves as non-Jews for various reasons. Like myself, they smuggled themselves back into the ghetto because they literally had no place else to go. All of us knew it was only a matter of time before the third deportation. Some tried desperately to obtain "Aryan" identity cards so they could escape the ghetto, but most could do little more than wait.

In the meantime, the daily terror continued unabated as the Gestapo, the SS, and their henchmen, the Ukrainian guards, tortured and killed almost at random. At one point, the SS announced that all Jews with valid visas for Palestine should come forward to be exchanged for ethnic Germans who lived in Palestine. Some sixty people were actually taken from this purgatory, sent halfway around the world, and reached Palestine safely. Soon after, another list of several hundred people with exit visas was compiled on orders of the SS and hopes soared. But this time their destination was a nearby trench and, after a thorough search for valuables, execution.

A group of sixty young men had been working for weeks at a secret Gestapo installation constructing large interconnecting straw mats. Among them was my cousin Abram, Uncle Hershel's son. Every day these sixty were picked up at the ghetto gates in the morning and brought back at night. Everyone was mystified as to what the mats were for and why they were such a closely guarded secret. One day the group was picked up in the morning and vanished from the face of the earth.

My hiding place in the attic was a safe haven. On several occasions the Jewish orderlies conducted dragnets for illegitimates in the ghetto, but they never came to search that building. I was able to rest there day after day. But even so, I was not growing healthy. I would get terribly tired at the slightest physical effort. It was the dead of winter, and the attic was cold and drafty. A deep hacking cough kept me from falling asleep at night. I also missed my family, and when alone, I often cried.

One morning Moniek and Lustig came to the attic a little earlier than usual, both smiling broadly. Lustig handed me a large wad of money and said that both their families decided to contribute to help me. That night they told me that the families had secured apartments in Warsaw and Aryan papers and would soon leave the ghetto. I asked how soon I had to leave the attic, and they said there was no hurry. I immediately arranged to send some money to my brother Eli in the munitions factory.

A few days later Moniek and Lustig helped me secure a basement room in a nearby building, vacated because the two people who lived there had been arrested by the Gestapo. That night I took my very meager belongings and moved to my new quarters. Moniek and Lustig were also able to obtain a food-ration card in my name, and to a certain extent, my presence in the ghetto was legitimized. But I had lost the relative safety of the Ackerman's attic and my existence became more precarious.

From the day I received my ration card, I was obliged to report daily at six a.m. to the employment section of the ghetto auxiliaries. The basic premise of life in the ghetto was that everyone there had to work and contribute in some way to the war effort to justify his or her right to live. The ghetto was constantly swept for undesirables who, when rounded up, were either shot on the spot or "resettled."

My greatest fear at the time was that I would get caught in a roundup of escapees from the munitions factory. I knew that if I was returned to my former bosses—Perkonique and Reich, the civilian Austrian engineers of Daimler/Benz—they would finish me off as an example to the others. And so each morning as I reported for work, I was quite uncertain whether I would return to the ghetto in the evening to live another day.

One morning, I was ordered to join a group of carpenters who worked on Szkolna Street near the munitions factory. The carpenters were highly skilled craftsmen whose official job was to prepare a place to house Jewish slave laborers from the nearby factory. In fact, they spent their time constructing luxurious pieces of furniture for the private use of the SS who were in charge of the ghetto. My job was to keep the place clean and assist the carpenters.

That day I saw SS Scharfurer Paul Nell for the first time. He drove up in a lorry with a Jewish man who obviously had been badly beaten sitting beside him. When they came into the shop, SS Sergeant Zlotosz, the shop supervisor, snapped to attention, saluted, and asked if he could be of help. Nell ordered him to get an armed Ukrainian guard from a nearby post. When Zlotosz returned with the guard, Nell asked for a shovel which he handed to the Jewish man. Nell then led them out to a field about fifty meters behind the carpenter's barrack and ordered the Jewish man to dig a hole of certain dimensions.

The people around me knew what was about to happen, because they had seen it before, but I had to watch from a window. It took some time to dig the hole in the already hardened ground. The Jewish man would periodically stop digging and fall to Nell's feet to plead for his life. Each time that happened, Nell would kick him in the face.

When the hole was deep enough, Nell took out his gun and shot the man several times.

I observed all this from the window. Even Sergeant Zlotosz seemed shocked and expressed his disapproval by shaking his head.

Nell dismissed the Ukrainian guard, returned to the shop, and ordered Sergeant Zlotosz to cover the grave.

On his way out, he took several candles from his pocket, and showed them to Sergeant Zlotosz. "This Jew won't steal from us anymore."

In the evening, we returned to the ghetto, that day's experience another memory.

And so, I existed from day to day doing all kinds of work for the powers that were, looking forward to the nights when I was able to spend time with Ella, Danka, Moniek, Lustig, and my other friends.

Winter came and with it came new forebodings. Some ghetto workers who were assigned to loading and unloading freight cars at the railroad station saw trains passing daily, traveling eastward loaded with Jews from all over Europe. The telltale signs of these railway coffins were the by-now-familiar little windows barred and crisscrossed with barbed wire. They were such a common sight in Poland that the Poles named them *"duszy-gubki"* or "soul-losers." Whenever it was possible to converse with the "passengers" of those trains, the answers were all the same—they believed they were traveling east to till the soil on Ukrainian farms.

One day such a train from Drancy outside Paris was derailed at the station in Radom. The Germans brought several wounded passengers to the ghetto and ordered them treated in the small hospital that still functioned there. After several weeks when they were all fully recovered, the Gestapo came in the night and shot them all.

One day in January 1943, I was forewarned by a friend that there was going to be a roundup of people like me who had worked in the munitions factory. I went to sleep that night with a feeling of total resignation. I was deathly afraid of going back. I knew that would be my end.

The next day I awoke to screams of *"Alle Juden Raus."*

I dressed in everything I possessed and left the basement room to join my fellow Jews for the next ordeal. It was the thirteenth of January 1943. The third deportation had begun.

The morning was cold but crisp and sunny. More than three thousand people were herded into a small square and once again began the game of who lives and who dies. Those whose work documents were no longer honored were herded into columns of one hundred, accompanied by indiscriminate shooting and beating. Some SS officers had come to the ghetto to make sure that "their" Jews, the ones they employed for their personal comfort and enrichment, would not be deported. At the same time a detail of SS searched the buildings with bloodhounds. Each time they found someone, they brought him out and shot him in sight of all.

I was very calm. I kept to the back of the crowd and contemplated my chances of getting out of this one. Then I spotted Ella in the crowd and started toward her.

When she saw me, she put her arms around me and sobbed uncontrollably. Her mother and sister had been admitted to the relative safety of the building where the Jewish orderlies' families were housed, but they would only admit two. Being the youngest, she opted to stay out.

I calmed her as much as possible and promised not to leave her, no matter what. Hand in hand, we walked to the back of the square where things were calmer. I now noticed several other young couples who had evidently also made up their minds to stay together and go with dignity.

One couple in their twenties I knew. His name was Garfinkel. His father was a good friend of my father's, and they lived near us. Garfinkel's girlfriend was uncommonly beautiful, but I remember I especially admired her demeanor, which seemed to say that no one would make her grovel. Both had backpacks strapped on and were munching on something. They were so beautiful, at peace, and obviously very much in love.

The sun was now a little higher and seemed to be sending its golden rays to brighten people's lives on such a cold day. But not for us, the damned. I could see free Polish people outside the ghetto hurrying by on their normal, everyday errands, casting furtive glances toward the ghetto and the special guards who were brought in for the deportation *aktion*. The gunfire from time to time only made them hurry faster.

I held on to Ella, and we decided to try to break out of the group destined for the trains and join the ranks of the workers selected to remain in the ghetto. But before we got close to the chooser of life and death, an SS guard grabbed Ella and yanked her away from me. She screamed, and he hit her in the face. He dragged her across the street and shoved her into a building.

I went limp and felt the crowd carry me along without any resistance, my will to fight for survival completely gone. Then after some time, I stumbled to the back of the crowd and sat on a rock to wait my turn and join the deportees. Once again I began to look forward to the end. I thought of my parents and my sister, Bluma, and I began feeling closer to them. In a way I was relieved that the end was approaching. I was tired of fighting.

I sat on that rock for a long time. The crowd in the square was beginning to thin out. The selection was nearing the end. I started walking back toward the selection table where several hundred people were still waiting to be processed.

Then I heard someone in the crowd call the name "Anoosh," the nickname of my cousin Harry, an orderly, who had evidently been brought in from the munitions factory to help with the deportation. I moved closer and spotted him standing in a strategic spot controlling the crowd with another orderly. I began to call his name just to let him know that I was there, but he would not turn around.

Seeing him aroused some hope and from some hidden source, my will to fight returned. I worked my way through the crowd until I was directly behind him, then I grabbed his jacket from the back and held it for dear life. He then turned and saw me. With his eyes, he motioned for me to stand behind him.

I surveyed the situation close up. Across the street, no more than ten yards away, stood a column of men who had evidently been chosen for some kind of work. If I could cross over the ten yards, my life would be spared, at least for a while. But it was not that simple. The SS was all over, supervising the *aktion*, and making sure, guns in hand, that everyone cooperated.

Then I saw that the SS man standing near Harry had a flask in his coat pocket. Every few minutes, he would holster his gun and take a deep swig. When he did this, he turned away so as not to be noticed by his superior down the street. At just the moment when it next happened, Harry pushed me across to the other group. Had the SS man noticed, we would have been shot then and there.

By twelve noon, it was all over. Sixteen hundred people were taken that day to the trains and transported to Treblinka for what the Germans called *Sonder Behandlung*, or "special treatment."

I remained in the now-reduced ghetto for several more weeks. One night two orderlies came to my basement room and told me to pack everything I owned. I was to be one of eighty men the SS required from the Radom ghetto to initiate the building of a new concentration camp in the nearby town of Blizyn.

CHAPTER 5

BLIZYN

As I looked around me at the other men selected to build the new concentration camp at Blizyn, I realized I had fallen in among the elite of the Radom ghetto. Among the eighty were ten ghetto orderlies, a doctor, an engineer, an accountant, and master craftsmen in the various trades—tailors, shoemakers, knitters, machine mechanics, electricians, and woodworkers. I was one of the few plain laborers.

We made the twenty-mile trip to Blizyn on a passenger train in a special car guarded by Polish policemen armed with carbines. We arrived at night and were herded through the dark into an empty, cold barrack by snarling, black-uniformed, white-gloved Ukrainian guards. They shoved in a couple of rusty pails for our toilet needs and locked the doors from the outside.

We spent a sleepless night wondering what was in store for us, each conjuring up his own vision of the new horrors ahead. In the morning, the doors opened, and we were chased out and lined up for our first roll-call count. The man facing us, the man seemingly in charge was SS Scharfurer Nell.

"You." He pointed to one of the ten orderlies, a man named Sol Mincberg. "Step forward."

Slowly, Sol stepped ahead, out of line.

"You are in charge," Nell said. "If you or any of your people fail to obey my orders, you will be severely punished. If anyone disobeys any camp rules, I'll see to it that he regrets it. Any escape attempt will be punished with the execution of several others."

Nell then strolled in front of us, his German shepherd dog beside him, resplendent in his uniform, preening with his God-like authority.

"As Jews," he said, "you should all be dead by now. But if you work hard and carry out orders promptly and efficiently, you may live for a while. At my discretion. First, you will surrender your belongings. Sergeant?"

At the sergeant's direction, the Ukrainian guards ordered us to undress completely, and we underwent a body search in the cold March weather. The guards lined us up single file, stark naked. We were told we could keep our shoes and belts but nothing else.

I had little else. The money and identity papers that I carried would do me little good here. But I still had pictures of all the members of my family as well as my friends. Those pictures were my greatest treasure, my last link to the world of my childhood. So while I stood on line, I desperately tried to stuff some of them into my shoe.

I was in the middle of the slow-moving line when Nell pulled a boy of no more than fourteen away from the table. In full view of all present, he ripped the boy's shoe away from him, pulled a handful of pictures from one toe, and held them aloft.

"I see that some of you were not listening earlier."

He tore the pictures into shreds and scattered them into the surrounding mud. He then unholstered his gun and shot the boy point-blank in the forehead.

"Perhaps now you will listen better."

When my turn at the table came, I gave up everything.

I grieved the rest of the day. I grieved terribly for the boy Nell had killed. I grieved for the pictures. But I grieved mostly because I had lost my last connection to humanity as I once knew it. I grieved because I had now become a nameless number.

On the next day after roll call, everyone was put to work to mend the barbed-wire fences surrounding the camp under the vigilant eyes of Ukrainian guards in the watchtowers. As we got our first look at the camp, we could see that we were not the first prisoners to have been housed there. There was something strange and frightening in the way the barracks looked. Each barrack had been wrapped on the outside with barbed wire from top to bottom. Barbed wire also blanketed the sloping ground for several feet on each side of the structure to prevent digging out. Even the large double doors were covered with wire on the outside, as were the little windows under the eaves that were much too high for anybody to reach. Also, the place was filled with the scent of carbolic acid, which seemed to come from the whitewashed walls.

We found the solution to those mysteries as soon as we started mending the barbed-wire perimeter. There we discovered that the local Polish people were eager to talk to us, even though it was strictly forbidden. After a number of different encounters with the outsiders, we were able to piece together the story.

When the Germans invaded Russia in 1941, they broke through the Russian defenses very quickly and took hundreds of thousands of Russian soldiers prisoner. The Germans then faced the problem of what to do with such great masses of prisoners. They couldn't possibly build POW camps for them all, let alone feed and house them for the duration.

In the end, they came up with a typical Nazi solution. Some of the prisoners, mostly Ukrainians, were integrated into the concentration camp network, and the rest were sent to places like Blizyn. Here thousands of Russian POWs were herded into the tightly wrapped barracks. Once they were inside, the barracks were closed up and sealed, and the prisoners were left to suffocate. Later their bodies were buried in trenches in a nearby forest.

Selected Russian prisoners were put in charge of each group, and after the liquidation was completed, they too were killed. After hearing this story, we all sank into a deep depression.

Soon after our arrival, transports of people began to come from ghettos and camps all over Poland. Kielce, Tomaszow,

Piotrkow, Czestochowa, Bialystok, all the great centers of Jewish life and culture. Along with the prisoners came machines of all kinds, looted from the ghettos. Factories for the manufacture of army uniforms, underwear, shoes, hats, knitted socks and sweaters were quickly established under the guidance of a civilian German manager, and the camp began to deliver a plethora of goods to the German army quartermaster.

Most of the Jews who had survived the ghetto deportations by working for the war effort were now being transferred into subcamps such as Blizyn and put under the direct control of the SS arm responsible for the execution of the Final Solution. This was a compromise between the Nazis who advocated killing all Jews immediately and those who preferred selecting the young and working them to death slowly.

In essence, Blizyn was a meat-grinding operation designed to suck every ounce of strength out of the inmates, then throw them away as they became useless. Our main enemy was hunger. Systematic starvation was the tool the Germans used to sap us of our will to live and resist, and we survived by doing whatever we could for extra food. Because I was one of the original eighty who later became camp administrators, I was sometimes able to get extra jobs that provided a little additional food.

The barrack that was my home was built during World War I as a stable. There were four hundred of us crammed into two continuous bunks stretching the whole length of either side. After evening roll call, we got a slice of bread with some watery soup, then the two large doors were locked from the outside. Several pails were placed in front for urinary needs. For any other needs, we were supposed to call the guard who would take us to the latrine, but no one ever dared. The doors were reopened at dawn for the morning roll call and the next day's work. That was our life, day in and day out. With few exceptions, the only social contact we had was after we were locked in and before we went to sleep.

Not long after the Blizyn camp was in full operation, a young boy named Stempel and I were assigned as caretakers for the barrack that housed the kitchen workers, the camp orderlies, and various other camp administrators. We were to clean up the place while they were out working, and they sometimes passed us some extra food for our efforts.

One afternoon, when our work for the day was done, one of the kitchen workers slipped us some potatoes. Stempel and I were forever hungry and knew that the fastest way to make potatoes edible was to cut thin slices and bake them on a hot surface. Because the orderlies who lived in this barrack were somewhat privileged, they were allowed to have a stove. Part of our job was to gather wood and use it to light the stove and to keep the barrack warm. Stempel and I started a good fire going, and as soon as the stove surface was hot, we sliced the potatoes and started eating them as fast as they became edible.

As we were blissfully munching on the potatoes, we felt a presence behind us. We turned and were face to face with Nell.

"Come with me," he said.

He took us to a toolshed manned by a boy we knew and handed Stempel and me each a shovel. He then led us to a hillside at the far end of the camp where many of his previous victims had been buried. His German shepherd, his faithful companion, was at his side.

I had risked death many times before, but I had never been this close to it. My first thought was that at least I got to walk to my own funeral. My second thought was to use the shovel to kill Nell and try to escape. But my upbringing in a culture of mutual responsibility held me back. I knew that I might get away with it but that the three thousand souls in the camp would be tortured and killed if I did.

Stempel had been whimpering for some time and now fell to Nell's knees.

"Please, please, Sir, forgive us. It'll never happen again, I swear it. Please don't—"

Without a word, Nell kicked Stempel in the mouth, then in the head. He was very matter of fact about it.

I pulled Stempel to his feet before Nell could kick him to death. When I had him upright with his arm over my shoulders, I whispered, "You know he enjoys this. Don't give him the pleasure."

We began walking again, me dragging the bleeding Stempel behind Nell. I was at peace with myself, looking forward to death as a relief, a liberation of sorts. Finally I would join my beloved family whom I missed so much. When we were close to the hillside, we heard someone running in our direction. Nell stopped and turned around. It was Sol Mincberg.

Mincberg completely ignored the two of us, as though we didn't exist, and joined Nell and his dog as we all walked toward the hillside. They got a bit ahead of us, but we could still hear an animated conversation taking place. Hope began to revive. Mincberg was the only person in the camp who had developed a relationship of sorts with Nell, and I knew that he was now doing his best to save our lives.

When we got to the hillside, Nell abruptly turned towards his nearby quarters without a word or a glance.

Mincberg let out a sigh of relief and said we owed our lives to the boy in the toolshed, who told him of our predicament. Mincberg was, of course, very modest and refused to let us hug and kiss him, and he strongly admonished us for being stupid.

"In the future," he said, "always use a lookout."

Since we were kept in very unsanitary conditions in a state of near starvation, it wasn't long before disease began to run through the camp. At first it was simply dysentery, then a terrible typhus epidemic set in.

There was a so-called "hospital barrack" in the camp where the sick were taken. There, the hospital director, Dr. David Weinapel, and his wife, Saba, made heroic attempts to save lives, attempts that proved futile since Nell didn't even provide them with aspirin. Nell had his own answer to the epidemics. On two occasions during roll call, Nell had the hospital raided, the sick killed, and all barracks fumigated. But none of this brought a halt to the typhus epidemic, and it wasn't long before the guards began to fall sick.

Because the camp administration was in the hands of people from Radom, most of whom I knew, it was possible for me to get extra food by doing odd jobs after work. Even so my health suffered. One day I was feeling particularly badly and decided to see Dr. Weinapel in the hospital barrack after work. He put his hand on my forehead and frowned.

"Expose your belly," he said.

I lifted my shirt and could immediately see the terrible frustration in his eyes. I looked down. My belly was covered with welts. I had the spotted typhus fever that Nell thought he had checked by killing the sick.

Dr. Weinapel laid a hand on my shoulder. "You know what this means?"

I nodded.

"I will try to save you," he said. "You know what my chances for success are."

"Just tell me what you want me to do, Doctor."

He told me to get undressed and join the others in the hospital. I was given a thin blanket and told to roll up my clothing and use that as a pillow. As soon as I lay down, I began to shake uncontrollably. My teeth began to rattle, and I felt the high fever in my body.

I closed my eyes, resigned from this world, and turned myself over once again to certain death. Before long, I began to drift in and out of consciousness.

At one point, I became aware that Nell was walking through the hospital barrack with his dog trotting obediently at his side. At his other side walked Dr. Weinapel.

"So what are you going to do now?" I heard Dr. Weinapel say. "Shoot them? It hasn't done you any good so far."

Sick as I was I couldn't believe my ears. This was the first time I ever heard a Jew standing up to a Nazi killer and getting away with it.

"It's not my job to keep Jews alive," Nell said.

"No, but it's your job to keep your own people alive, isn't it? And you know that several Ukrainians and your own SS are down with the disease. Remember, not even you are immune."

"I know these things, Doctor, and I will do what I must."

"Well, I'm telling you the only way to keep yourselves alive is to get me the medicines I need. Either that, or kill every last Jew in the camp. And you may as well start with me."

Of course, I knew Nell needed Dr. Weinapel more than ever. He was vicious enough to kill every one of us, but he also needed to keep the factories going. In the end, he nodded. "Give me a list of the medicines you need, and I'll try to get them."

Fate had again shined upon me. The next day, Saba injected something into my arm. The following day when Dr. Weinapel came to check on me, my fever had broken. I was very weak, but alive.

"I overheard your conversation with Nell," I said to Dr. Weinapel as he was leaning over me.

"Oh?"

"You stood up to him to save us. I have never seen such courage. You are a hero."

"I am a doctor." Dr. Weinapel patted my hand. "But for now, I think you should go out for the roll call. Nell is still in charge, and he may change his mind."

I was so weak that I was barely able to walk the hundred meters to the field where the roll calls were held. Two boys had to grab me and hold me while the counting and reporting took place. When it was over, the rest formed columns and marched to their respective workplaces led by the assigned orderlies. I collapsed on the ground. I was lying there waiting to accumulate enough strength to make it back to the hospital when I felt someone help me up. I turned and saw Sol Mincberg, the inmate head of the camp.

"Steady, now boy," he said. "We'll get you somewhere warm and safe."

Slowly, with careful affection, he walked me toward the camp kitchen. When we got there, he sat me down on a bench among the women potato-peelers, then called the kitchen orderly.

"Take care of this one until he gets his strength back," he said.

I sat there completely exhausted with tears of gratitude streaming down my face. Perhaps there was a God after all. And maybe, just maybe, I was destined to survive.

The following day after roll call, Sol Mincberg looked me up again and asked if I felt any better. Again he supported me, this time for the longer distance to the so-called Hall of the Mechanics. Once inside the hall, he led me to the section occupied by a group of sewing-machine mechanics and sat me down on a workbench.

"You have a new worker," he said. "His name is Yossek. Treat him well."

Once again tears of gratitude streamed. Mechanic was one of the most sought-after jobs in the camp. It was impossible to get unless one had experience, and I had none.

Once again, Sol Mincberg, who was neither my friend nor my relative—in fact I barely knew him in Radom—had given me the gift of life.

It was after I became a mechanic that I began to find the opportunities to apply the smuggling skills I had learned in the ghetto in Radom. By knowing who was bribable and who was not, I was able to barter clothing made in the factories and sell it over the fence to the Poles for food. I was part of a group of eight mechanics who worked together, smuggled together and bunked together. One of them in particular, Moses Bilke, became my smuggling partner while the others worked.

The leader of our group was a young man named Reuben. He was of medium height, with dark features and flashing hazel eyes. I can picture him so clearly, that if I had any artistic ability, I could draw an exact likeness of him, even now, more than fifty years later.

In the evenings, after the barrack was locked, our group formed a circle on the bunk, and Reuben passed out the extra food we earned that day. Then, while the rest of us ate greedily, he always took a part of his share and gave it to someone who needed it more desperately than he. When I finished eating, I always felt ashamed of myself that I couldn't do the same. But I could not help it.

One evening, as we were about to begin eating, an inmate named David came by to say hello. We all knew David well. He was older, in his thirties, had a Chassidic background, and was well versed in the Torah. He always carried himself with a certain integrity that comes with knowledge and education, even when he was simply begging for food, as he was tonight.

It was an unwritten rule in the barrack that no one was supposed to interfere when the mechanics were about to eat. But instead of ignoring David, Reuben made us widen the circle and admit him. He then gave David an equal portion when he distributed the food. There was some grumbling, but nobody dared contradict Reuben.

David ate part of his portion then rose.

"You must excuse me," he said. "Good fortune like this I must share with my friend Jan."

"Jan?" Bilke said.

"Yes," David said. "He is the Jan from Bialystok. He was a famous Russian radio announcer there."

When it was time to go to sleep, David returned to our bunk.

"I thought I might repay your kindness, if you will permit me."

"Of course," Reuben said, "but how?"

In response, David began to sing the most beautiful, wistful Chassidic songs. It had been so long since I heard music that I had forgotten the power it could have. Very quickly, I found myself weeping uncontrollably.

"If you please," David said when he was done, "Jan also has something to offer."

Then from across the barrack came a voice.

"This is Jan, coming to you this evening from Blizyn with the latest news."

Jan's voice was rich and cultured, and he spoke with great authority. The whole barrack became still as Jan's melodic voice rang out and lifted us temporarily out of purgatory into another world. Unhaltingly, Jan spoke of great battles fought in the past, and new battles to be fought in the future. He spoke of the great defeat inflicted on the Nazis, the enemy of mankind, at Stalingrad. Then in a measured, convincing voice, he warned the barbarous Nazis that an angry world was coming to crush them for their crimes against humanity.

"And to those of you suffering under the boot of the Nazis, I say, hold on at all cost. The world is even now coming to your rescue."

As I laid my head down on the hard board, I thanked God for such a beautiful evening. And I thanked Reuben for having made it possible.

Not long after, new transports began to arrive, and among them was a boy named Jacob. He came from Czestochowa and was assigned to my barrack. He was an attractive boy with dark brooding features. I became friends with him and he eventually bunked next to me. After lights out, we would share our memories of home and family and of days gone by. One night he shared a terrible secret with me.

Jacob, along with some members of his family had been deported from Czestochowa to Treblinka in the summer of 1942. When they arrived, about half the people in his car were dead from heat and lack of water. The rest were unloaded on the ramp and chased with whips and dogs to a field, where they had to undress. At that point, an SS man picked him and a few other healthy-looking young boys and told them to step out. They were taken to join the group that serviced the Treblinka death camp facility. The rest of the people were sent to a sealed barrack, gassed, and cremated.

It was Jacob that introduced me for the first time to the horrible truth at the heart of the Holocaust—that death was not a by-product of the camps. Death was the reason the camps existed. The whole camp system was a swift and efficient genocide machine conceived and built by this German superrace of psychopaths.

He taught me a song which the slaves in Treblinka sang in the barracks at night after work. I only recall a fraction of the lyrics, but I will never forget the haunting melody.

Treblinka, there
For every Jew a final resting place.
Whoever goes there, remains there
Remains forever.
Whoever gets there,
Our mothers, fathers,
Sisters, brothers
They are all poisoned
And that is their end.

After he had learned the truth, Jacob escaped from Treblinka by burying himself in a truck full of clothing and other loot taken from the victims and made his way back to Czestochowa, where he still had close family. When he arrived, he told the others what he had seen.

No one believed him, not even his own father. Out of anger and frustration, Jacob volunteered for Blizyn. He stopped telling the story except to people like me, whom he befriended and liked. He said I was one of the few who believed him.

After I heard Jacob's story, I could no longer hold back the anguish I felt about the deportation of my loved ones, could no longer delude myself about their fate. I understood the bitter truth at last—it all fit in. I had abandoned my dearest family to a horrendous death. I began saying the Kaddish daily and mourned my family all over again, as if they had just expired. But I became more determined than ever to fight for survival.

It was not long after this that Nell stood before us at roll call.

"Last night one of you escaped from this camp. You know what that means."

Although there were occasional successful escapes, most prisoners were brought back to camp by Polish bounty hunters. Even though the preponderance of the Polish population outside the barbed wire were themselves brutalized by the Germans, they still cooperated with the Nazis against their Jewish neighbors. Many would denounce escaped Jews to the Nazis without asking for a reward. Even the powerful Polish underground, who harried the Germans from their hideouts in the dense forests around Blizyn (and who were heavily supported by the Allies), would routinely shoot escaped Jews on sight.

All of this meant there were few attempted escapes, even though there were opportunities. Behind the barbed-wire, life was hell on earth, but we still helped and respected each other. Outside the wire, we were literally hated by friend and foe alike.

And, of course, for each escape, there were immediate reprisals. Nell would walk among us at roll call and occasionally, without warning, pull a prisoner out and force him to kneel, then shoot him in the temple.

That day, when Nell began walking down the row behind me, I closed my eyes. I heard him drawing closer then stopping near me. I winced.

Then I heard a cry of, "No, please!"

He had chosen Jacob, who was right behind me.

I dared to look and saw Jacob kneeling at Nell's feet. "No, please, don't do this. See?" Jacob rolled back his sleeve and flexed his arm. "See? I'm still strong yet. I can still do a lot of hard work."

Nell pulled his pistol.

"No, please," Jacob wailed. "I must live, I must tell, I must live, I must—"

I looked away just as Nell pulled the trigger. I was standing close enough to be spattered by Jacob's blood.

Later that day, I helped bury him and said Kaddish over his grave. I promised that if I survived, I would tell the truth, for as long as I lived to anyone who would listen.

Despite the risk of escape and the certainty of retribution, some did try to get away. One escape was especially daring. On a day when Nell was away from camp, a group of ten people accompanied by two orderlies and a Ukrainian guard presented themselves at the main gate with a typewritten order signed by Nell to perform a job outside the wire. There was some question at the gate as to the validity of the order, but the guards manning the gate that day, afraid of Nell's reaction, let the work party through.

When Nell returned and found the ten people missing at roll call, he was so furious that he ordered two rucksacks filled with rocks, then had the gate guards strap them to their backs and hop for hours until they were half-dead. He also executed five prisoners in reprisal.

On another occasion, a young woman appeared outside the barbed wire where most of the trading took place and asked to have a man named Bolek, from Tomaszow, brought to the fence. I was present at the time, and I knew Bolek casually. He was an extremely handsome young man constantly seen in the company of a very pretty young girl also from

Tomaszow. I immediately dispatched a boy to fetch him. When he arrived, the young woman outside the fence passed a piece of paper to him, and they chatted for a minute or so.

Suddenly there was a commotion, and I heard dogs barking.When I turned, I saw several SS men with leashed dogs running towards the fence from the outside. The young woman panicked and raced away through a field in the direction of a nearby forest. The SS brought her down with several well-aimed shots.

I was later told by Wanda, my main Polish contact in the smuggling operation, that the son of one of the women who traded with us over the fence ran around the camp perimeter and notified the SS in the front office of the young woman stranger who came to see a Jewish prisoner. The young woman killed that day turned out to be Bolek's sister, who lived on Aryan papers outside the wire. She came to see her brother and for that she paid with her life.

Soon after this happened, Bolek and his female friend disappeared from the camp. Their escape was very baffling because no break could be found in the fence and neither of them worked outside. Special dogs were brought in to sniff all around the camp perimeter, and they eventually found the escape route. The couple was somehow privy to the location of an underground system of canals that ran throughout the camp. They went down into the canal by lifting and replacing one of the manholes, then followed an underground route that took them outside.

Nell immediately ordered Polish masons to come in and seal all possible entrances or exits of this elaborate underground canal system. The sealing was done under the direction of Engineer Baum, one of the original eighty from Radom, and supervised personally by Nell. They made doubly sure that the exit was barred by a very thick wall of cement. After this was done, Nell executed several people in reprisal for the escape and considered the matter closed.

But it wasn't. Engineer Baum was a daily visitor to the Hall of the Mechanics because of his obvious need to be in touch with the building craftsmen who worked out of there. One day he contacted Reuben and had a long chat with him. That evening Reuben disclosed to us the gist of their conversation. Baum had directed the sealing of all entrances to the underground canal except one, and that one was located in the Hall of the Mechanics directly under one of our workbenches.

In return for this information, Baum asked for and received Reuben's solemn promise to be included in any escape attempt.

From that day on, Bilke and I would take night duty at the main sewing hall, which gave us time and undisturbed access to the canal opening under the workbench. For weeks, Bilke and I worked in the canal with hammer and chisel on the thick mortar of the sealed exit. The plan was to chisel away the mortar without breaking through, (guard patrols checked the spot frequently) leaving the wall thin enough so it would collapse with the application of a little pressure from the inside.

That job was accomplished successfully, and there came a day when Bilke and I announced to the others that we had an open exit out of the camp that could be used at any time we wanted.

From that day on, we began to discuss how and when.

"Now that we have an open escape route, we must use this advantage carefully," Reuben said.

"You mean you must use it carefully," said Mr. Orenstein, an older man from Piotrkow. "Escape is not for me.

I'd only be a hindrance to you and slow you down. Besides where can we run to?"

"We have our sister and our father here," one of the Belzycki brothers from Tomaszow said. "Even if we could leave them, Nell would surely kill them."

"How can we wait?" Mendel, a young man from Radom said. "We have to leave this hellhole. Even if they lose the war soon, they will never let us live. Staying is suicide."

"Leaving may be suicide, too," I said. "Of all the prisoners who tried to escape, how many do you know who weren't brought back? Only a handful. And for all we know, that handful is laying dead somewhere."

"As of now, we're not starving here," Bilke said. "And on the outside things are changing. Let's wait and see."

Reuben nodded. "Let's keep this to ourselves and discuss it from time to time. If an emergency arises, we'll know what to do."

One day in the summer of 1943, a transport arrived from Radom. Bilke and I knew that the new arrivals would be stripped of all their belongings, which would be taken to a camp warehouse for processing and eventual shipment to Germany.

So we struck a deal with several Ukrainian guards whom we had done business with before. Bilke and I stationed ourselves at a strategic spot, and as the guards rode by with a load of confiscated luggage, they made sure that a couple of valises fell off the wagon, where we collected them. By the end of the day, we had about a dozen pieces of luggage stored away in a hiding place in the mechanic's hall. Later, we would sort this loot and trade it to the Poles on the outside for food and vodka to pay off the Ukrainian guards.

Before we had a chance to sort the contents of the luggage, though, Bilke decided to hunt for some socks that might fit him. The first valise he opened contained exactly what he needed, so he took several pair, one of which he put on then and there.

That afternoon, when the new arrivals from Radom had been put through disinfection and other unpleasant initiations, they were assigned to a barrack in camp. After roll call, I was eager to see if I knew any of them, so Bilke and I made our way across the camp. As soon as we entered their barrack, I came face to face with Aamek Birenbaum, one of my classmates from Miss Soboll's clandestine school.

After a heartfelt greeting, Aamek took us to see his mother, Salka, and his eight-year-old brother, Davidek. They were in a state of shock after their camp entry experience, which was every bit as brutal as mine. But my presence lifted their spirits somewhat, especially when I assured them they could have done much worse than Blizyn. We embraced and kissed, and my spirits lifted as well. It was such a joy to see a young child again, especially one as smart and charming as Davidek. I introduced Bilke as the sharpest over-the-wire trader in camp, and we settled down to tell our stories.

I told them of my near-capture in the small ghetto and how I found my way into the work force at Blizyn. I knew that Aamek's father, Motek, had been drafted into the Polish army, then taken prisoner by the Russians when they attacked Poland in 1939. Aamek told me that they knew nothing of his whereabouts except that he was sent to Siberia soon after he was captured. Aamek and his mother survived the deportations in Radom by working at a German Wehrmacht supply depot, and Davidek got special permission from a high-ranking German army officer to help his mother at work.

Just before this happy meeting ended, Salka took me aside.

"Yossek," she said, "do you know your friend is wearing Aamek's socks?"

"What?"

"I don't know how it could be, but I am sure those socks are Aamek's"

The following day, Bilke and I checked the looted suitcases and found two that belonged to the Birenbaums. Bilke didn't even hesitate when I suggested we return them. And so it was that the Birenbaums were the only people in the entire camp to have kept, in a roundabout way, at least some of their belongings.

At my next meeting with Aamek, I shared Jacob's story with him. Aamek flatly refused to believe it.

In addition to trading across the wire for food, we also traded with the locals for news. That is how we heard of the Nazi defeat at Stalingrad that so buoyed our hopes. And that is how we kept abreast of the events that shaped our lives.

The Nazi solution to the "Jewish problem" had already been largely implemented by the time of Stalingrad. The gas chambers had claimed most of their victims, and those of us still alive, the young and healthy, were being systematically worked to death. But after the Russians denied the Nazis the swift victory they expected, the Nazis realized that the war would become protracted. And since their main work force was in the army, fighting an ever-stronger coalition of enemies, they began to preserve their slave labor for the war industry. The Nazis remained uncompromising in the total destruction of the Jewish elderly and children, but young men were increasingly seen as an important resource.

We could see the results of this shift in policy around us as our supply of food and medicine improved. Even Nell became less brutal as time went by. We also saw how Germans who were part of the occupation force in Poland were sent to the Russian front as a form of punishment. Some Germans even committed suicide when they were informed that they were to be transferred.

But the most important change in policy came in the beginning of 1944, when a new contingent of SS men arrived, headed by an officer named Heller, and took over the administration of the camp. We never saw Nell or his crew again.

Oberscharfurer Heller was a very tall and handsome man who walked with a slight limp due to wounds he received on the Russian front. The mere fact that he was a military man rather than a trained killer sent our hopes soaring, and those hopes were soon realized. The climate in the camp improved.

One day, not long after Heller took over, Bilke and I received a message from Wanda. She needed a number of sewing-machine parts for which she gave original Singer serial numbers. She offered twenty loaves of bread and whatever it would take to bribe the guards if she could get the parts promptly. Reuben recognized that this was a great bonanza and immediately sent two men to search for the parts in the warehouse where hundreds of sewing machines were stored. The parts were found, and Wanda was notified that the deal could be made at any time.

As was customary at such events, we placed a string of lookouts in all the strategic spots. Then Bilke and I tossed the bag of parts over the fence to Wanda, and she tossed the bread back. We caught the loaves and stacked them in a wheelbarrow. It was only after we had started back to the Hall of the Mechanics that we realized Heller had seen the entire transaction from a distant bridge that ran between the lower end of the camp and the SS quarters. We rushed into the hall and hid the bread in a hollowed tabletop the carpenters had made to hide just such contraband. Then Bilke and I shed our clothing to blend in with the rest.

Less than a minute later, the shop foreman yelled "*Achtung!*" and Heller strode in with two armed SS guards. All he saw by that time was locksmiths, roofers, carpenters, machine mechanics, and electricians seemingly hard at work. Heller walked up to the foreman. "Where is the bread?" he said. "Where are the smugglers?"

The foreman said nothing.

Heller grabbed the small man by his hair and effortlessly lifted him up to his eye level.

"Where is the bread?" he shouted. "Where are the smugglers?"

The foreman fainted. Heller let go of his hair, and the man collapsed like a sack of bones. Heller looked with disgust at the shapeless body at his feet, then stepped over it, and began to slowly walk around the hall. His two companions were at the door, their guns ready. We were still at full attention.

As he walked, Heller paused before each one of us and studied us intently, but he had been too far away to be sure, and Bilke and I were well schooled at keeping a straight face. Finally he walked to the center of the hall and faced us.

"Not ten minutes ago, I watched two of your number trade contraband material over the fence for bread," he said. "The two were of medium height, dark hair, young and slim. One was in a red sweater, the other wore a gray tunic. I saw them come in here, so I know you all know who they are. If the two scoundrels come forward, the rest of you can go back to work in peace."

Heller paused, clearly expecting for the group to pull the guilty out of the ranks to save themselves.

No one spoke. No one moved.

Heller's shock could not have been greater than ours. For the first time, we were defying an SS officer.

Heller walked over to the guards at the door and ordered one of them to get more help. Then he paced back and forth in front of us.

"You have clearly made your choice," he said after a moment. "It no longer matters who the smugglers are or where the bread is hidden. In a few minutes, you will all be shot."

Moments later we heard soldiers trotting in place outside. When the large double door was opened, a squad of black-uniformed, white-gloved Ukrainian guards armed with rifles and billy clubs marched in, lined up beside Heller, and came to attention. Their leader saluted and reported ready for orders. "*Zum-Befehl!*" he shouted.

If Heller wanted to terrify us, he made the right choice. Of all the guards in the camp, the Ukrainians were the most vicious. They had been handpicked by the SS and trained to do the dirty work, the work which even the SS found loathsome.

Heller stepped forward once again, a smile on his face. "You see who you are facing. Will you hand over the smugglers now?"

Not a soul moved.

Heller's face turned purple. "You ungrateful Jewish bastards!"

Foam appeared at the corners of his mouth. "Haven't I increased the food rations? Haven't I seen to it that you have coal for the barrack stoves? And this is how you repay me, by breaking the camp rules in broad daylight? And then you dare make me face a conspiracy? A conspiracy by Jews? Impossible!"

At that he gave the go-ahead to the Ukrainians.

The Ukrainians formed two lines and then forced us to run the gauntlet. As we did, they rained blows down on us with clubs and rifle butts. The cement floor of the hall soon turned red and slippery from the blood. At one point, the man in front of me fell, and I was forced to stomp over him, as the guards on either side clubbed my head, ribs, and kidneys. Two or three times, my knees buckled under me and I fell. The guards continued kicking me until somebody picked me up to face more blows.

Finally, a whistle blew, and the carnage stopped.

Heller walked over to an elderly man, a master roofer whom we all admired for his kindness, and placed his gun behind his ear.

"You have five seconds, who are the smugglers?"

A barely audible whisper came out.

"I don't know, Sir."

Heller shoved the old man back into the ranks and ordered everyone outside. Then he had us lined up against the wall of the building, with the Ukrainians behind us. We heard the guns being cocked.

I remember waiting for the shots to ring out. I was too numb to care. All I wanted was to fall down, even if it was forever.

Once again Heller's voice rang out. "This is your last chance."

Several people fell to the ground, unable to support their weight any longer. We had reached the limit of human endurance.

We waited.

"*Abtreten!*" Heller ordered. Then he and his cohorts stalked off without a word.

We were left brutally beaten, completely exhausted, but alive. Thanks to the courage and kindness of the others in that hall, I had survived certain death once again.

On the way up to his quarters, Heller stopped off at the camp kitchen and ordered double portions of food for all workers in the Hall of the Mechanics for that day.

One morning in the spring of 1944, a long column of civilian refugees was admitted to the camp at Blizyn—ethnic Germans escaping from the advancing Russian armies in the east. From conversations with them, we learned of the ferocity of the Russian military assault. When Hitler had unleashed his armies against Russia, almost three years earlier, he ordered them to fight what he called a "total war."

We had heard of the results of that war on the Russian prisoners who died here at Blizyn. Now as they retreated, the Germans were reaping the whirlwind of their brutality. In their counteroffensives, the Russians took few prisoners, and those they took were treated no better than the Germans had treated them.

Clearly, the day of reckoning was approaching. It was no longer a question whether Hitler would be defeated, only when. Still the Germans fought fiercely for their *Fuehrer* because he had quite purposely made them coresponsible for the heinous crimes they had committed on his orders. They knew that the wrath of the world would exact a terrible retribution on them as well as their leaders for the abominable crimes they had committed.

Though it was a thrill for us in Blizyn to see defeated Germans in our midst, the thrill was not without an edge of fear. The Russian armies were closing in, and every surviving Jew knew full well that the Nazis would kill us before they went down in defeat.

Suddenly an evacuation fever seized the camp. Rumors started flying about our transfer to different destinations in Germany. As if to confirm the rumors, truckloads of striped clothing, such as worn in German concentration camps, arrived and were distributed to the inmates.

Every night my small group of mechanics discussed our plans for the escape. Now that Heller was the commander, retribution for escape was no longer as severe. The problem was to choose a moment when our chances for survival outside the camp were great enough to justify the risk.

The Russians were no more than thirty miles away, but on the other bank of the Vistula River, and we had to survive until they arrived.

In the end we decided our best hope was to escape as soon as night fell and march about twenty miles east to a forest, that according to information we received from the Poles, was under the control of the Polish underground army, the A.K. Once there, we'd wait until the Russians crossed the Vistula and continued their assault.

The plan seemed reasonable to all except Reuben.

"What happens if the Russians decide not to cross the river for several months?" he said.

"They have the Germans on the run now," Mr. Orenstein said. "They must take advantage of the serious weaknesses in the German defenses."

"Our greatest enemies are the Poles outside the wire," I said. "How many times have we seen them bring back escaped Jews just for the bounty of some sugar?"

"Their attitude has to change," Bilke said. "Now that the war is almost over, they must be thinking of what the Russians will do to them for cooperating with the Nazis."

"Listen," Reuben said, "let's ask Wanda. We all trust her. Let's hear what she has to say."

The next evening, Bilke and I assumed the night shift, and in the dead of night asked the Ukrainian guards to fetch Wanda for a meeting. Such meetings usually took place at the back gate of the camp—the two Ukrainian guards stationed there were almost always on the take. But this time Wanda actually invited us to come to her house. The gate was unlocked, and one of the guards accompanied Bilke and me.

Wanda lived in a modest house no more than a hundred yards from the camp. Her husband Vladek was with her and her two small children were asleep in an adjoining room. She served some bread and cheese and put a bottle of vodka on the table.

It seemed like a lifetime since I had seen the inside of a real home. The many religious objects displayed prominently all over the house made me feel a little uncomfortable, but I had absolute trust in Wanda's integrity. She was a true and concerned Christian. We each had a drink of vodka then passed the rest of the bottle to the guard.

I laid out our escape plan to Wanda and Vladek. Then Bilke spoke of our reservations.

"What are our chances of making it to the forest in one night?" he said. "And what will happen to us once we reach the forest?"

Wanda crossed herself and began to mutter prayers. "I will let Vladek answer," said Wanda. Vladek poured himself a stiff drink and downed it.

"You will have no problem making it to the forest sanctuary in one night. Your problems will start once you get there. You see—"

"They will kill you as soon as they discover you. In God's name"—Wanda crossed herself—"go with the Germans. Go to Auschwitz, go wherever they send you, as God is my witness, but don't escape. If you do, you are as good as dead."

"I am an officer of the A.K.," Vladek said. "I know that we are under unwritten orders to keep our country free of Jews. The enforcement of these orders are up to the local commanders. In this area, you don't stand a chance."

I sat with my mouth open for a long moment. Freedom was only thirty miles away, and we still couldn't reach it.

"Doesn't it make a difference that the war is almost over?" I said at last. "The Russians will be here soon."

"Yes," Vladek said, "and our fight against the Russians and any surviving Jews will start as soon as we are rid of the Germans."

Wanda shook her head and kept mumbling, "*Jezus Chrystus, Jezus Chrystus*, have pity on these unfortunate people."

There was nothing more to say. Bilke motioned to the half-drunk guard that it was time to go back, back to the relative safety of our concentration camp.

Several days later, on a beautiful, sunny day in June 1944, a special detachment of German SS arrived in Blizyn, surrounded the camp, and relieved the Ukrainian guards. Commander Heller spoke to us as we stood at attention for our last roll call.

"Prisoners," he said, "the Third Reich needs your labor. Thanks to the *Fuehrer*'s generosity, you will all be spared and sent to Germany to fill the needs of German industry. As under my command, you will be treated decently as long as you work conscientiously. You will wear the striped clothing on your journey which will help identify you as experienced laborers for the Reich."

After roll call, fifty people were chosen to remain behind and clean up, among them Sol Mincberg and Engineer Baum. The rest of us were formed into columns of one hundred and marched to the local railroad station where a long freight train was waiting to receive us. Tucked away in a wire mesh pocket on the side of each car was a bill of lading.

The destination clearly read "AUSCHWITZ."

CHAPTER 6

BIRKENAU

The following morning the train rolled into the infamous receiving ramp at Birkenau.

Through a crack between the boards of the boxcar, I could see row upon row of barbed wire, studded with white porcelain electricity conductors. Beyond the wire, on either side of the tracks, stood hundreds of barracks in perfectly symmetrical order. Guard towers dotted the landscape every hundred yards. The sky was blue, the sun bright, the day was balmy, and the world seemed at peace and beautiful. From afar came the strains of music. I could see prisoners in striped clothing at a distance, and more on the ramp. The ones on the ramp seemed bored. The whole area was surrounded by SS guards with dogs straining at their leashes.

The train screeched to a halt. Our guards hopped off the car, and we heard a harsh command, *"Raus! Raus! Raus!"* Eager to show how strong and agile we were, we jumped out of the cars with military precision and lined up exactly, as for a routine camp count off. We didn't have to relinquish personal belongings because we came from a concentration camp and didn't have any.

Heller was down the ramp chatting amiably with other SS officers. It was clear that they were deciding the fate of the three thousand newcomers. We were all in our prime, few older than forty-five or younger than fifteen, except for nine-year-old Davidek Birenbaum. Heller and the Auschwitz SS officers walked closer and casually gave us a once-over, then one of the officers went to a guard and gave him orders. Immediately we were given orders to march. First the women then the men. The Birkenau prisoners on the ramp relaxed and smiled. No selection was going to take place that morning. Some whispered the good news to the newcomers. All of us were to be housed in the camp as potential laborers.

Entering the camp was like landing on a new planet. Jacob's stories about Treblinka had stripped me of my illusions about the Nazis, and I had heard about the Birkenau genocide factory at Auschwitz. But nothing prepared me for the absolute order and efficiency of the place. As we marched toward the "sauna" for the camp entry procedure, we passed the two main killing facilities, located on either side of the railroad tracks about half a mile from the arrival ramp. They could have been giant bakeries or laundries, except for the smell of the thick black smoke belching from their chimneys and the double row of electrified barbed-wire fence surrounding them.

Clearly the Germans had learned from their experiences with the comparatively crude genocidal facilities in eastern Poland and built these death factories for the utmost efficiency.

Because I knew the Germans prized skilled workers, I made sure I stayed close to my mechanic friends, especially Bilke. In our time in Blizyn, Bilke and I had formed a very close friendship and learned to rely on each other. Bilke once told me that, in the village where he was born and lived, there was only a cheder, and he only knew how to read and write Hebrew. But he had worked at the mechanic's trade as an apprentice since he was ten years old and was one of the best mechanics in Blizyn.

No one told us what to expect when we entered the sauna, and even we veterans became disoriented. From the moment I passed the entry door, burly SS guards with clubs and whips rained blows on me, forcing me to move fast. First came a thorough and brutal body search, then all my hair was clipped, then I was shoved under an ice-cold shower, after which I was doused with disinfectant—all in record-breaking time while I held on to my belt with one hand and my shoes with the other.

After the shower, we were chased into a large hall where stacks of striped clothing were piled high. At a table behind each stack stood an inmate worker who dispensed one article of clothing in assembly-line fashion. All this was done to the accompaniment of SS men screaming, *Schnell!*

Schnell! and landing blows on whomever they could reach. It was enough to daze even the toughest.

As I passed through the clothing room, I noticed a couple of familiar faces from Radom. They had disappeared years before and were long presumed dead by their families. Throughout the procedure, they kept their eyes down and never broke their work rhythm, but they definitely recognized friends and relatives among us. I also noticed that Bilke, who was just ahead of me, spoke briefly with one of the sauna boys.

When we got to the end of the line and received our new outfits, we were chased to a clearing outside, where we were finally rid of the SS overseers and were able to dress. Naturally, bartering began immediately because no one received the proper size clothing.

When we were all more or less dressed, we lined up in marching order and a "Capo," a camp inmate policeman, took control of us. Just before we left the sauna perimeter, the boy who had spoken to Bilke came out and talked with him for a moment again. I suspected that by doing so he was breaking the rules and risking severe punishment.

The column marched out of the clearing and along a road that led towards the many barracks I had seen on arrival. On the way, we passed two more gas chambers with the telltale chimneys belching smoke. As we marched, Bilke managed to tell me that the sauna boy was his best childhood friend, Boris. In the quick, hushed conversation on the sauna premisses, Boris told him that after a short stay in quarantine, we would probably be moved to Camp D. If and when that happened, Bilke was to report to one Capo Janek for a job and mention his name. Bilke pointed me out as his friend and got approval to ask for two jobs.

I had no idea what these jobs might entail but suspected that once again a chance encounter with fate had spelled the difference between life and death.

After a short march, we entered Camp A, the quarantine compound for newcomers and were lined up in front of several "scribes." Each of us received a number that was tattooed on the left underarm and sewn on a patch that was displayed prominently on the left breast of the striped prison jacket. After each number was a colored triangle. Red denoted detention for political reasons, green was for criminals, black was asocial or Gypsy, pink was homosexual, and purple was Jehovah's Witness.

I got number B-1477 with a yellow triangle pointing downward. This meant that I was a Jew, the lowliest of the low in the eyes of my SS captors.

That number was to be my sole identification for the rest of the war. Aside from my belt and shoes, I had nothing to connect me to my pre-Auschwitz life, not even a name.

Totally exhausted and bewildered, we newcomers were finally permitted to enter a barrack. As we walked in single file, each of us was handed a tin soup plate and spoon, which the barrack orderly told us to guard with our lives. Then we were greeted by a well-dressed, well-fed prisoner whose armband read "*Blockealteste*." The blockeldest gave us a short speech in German that left us thoroughly convinced that the slightest deviation from routine would bring on immediate punishment, the likes of which we could never imagine. With this speech ringing in our ears, and a bit of watery soup and a slice of bread in our hungry bellies, we went to sleep in our new home, the crown jewel death camp and killing center of the new German order.

A few days later, we were subjected to our first "selection." Like everything else in Auschwitz, this was a barbarous procedure performed in a routine and very orderly manner. All prisoners in the barrack lined up in front of the bunks, single file, stark naked. Then an SS officer wearing a white smock over his uniform—to give him the aura of a doctor, I suppose—walked among us accompanied by an armed guard, the blockeldest, and the blockscribe. From time to time, the officer would nod toward a prisoner, and the scribe would write down his number. That prisoner was then condemned to the gas chamber.

The blockeldest had already explained the Auschwitz code to us. When your number was chosen, you remained calm. That way you sometimes had a couple of weeks before you were collected by special trucks for the Cremo. Otherwise a much more terrible end would be meted out right on the spot.

Many of the prisoners selected that day had no problem remaining quiet. They were Hungarian Jews who had been taken from relative comfort at home straight to this hellhole. Some became suicidal after they learned the meaning of the smoke-belching chimneys and the fate of loved ones from whom they were separated on the arrival ramp. They were quite willing to be selected to put an end to it.

To my great sorrow and pain, one of the last ones to be selected that day was the nine-year-old Davidek Birenbaum.

The women from Blizyn were housed in Camp B, which had a common electrified, double-barbed wire fence with Camp A. A few days after our arrival, I and some others risked getting close enough to that fence to talk with the women when the walking guard patrol was out of sight. The sight of our women gave me a crushing, humiliating feeling. The first one at the fence, on the women's side, was Salka, Aamek and Davidek's mother.

She looked most pitiful. Her hair had been clipped off with a few painful snips of a large scissor, leaving her head scarred and ugly. And though she was a tall woman, she was wearing a short garment that made her look pathetic.

But her thoughts were not on how she looked.

"Yossek, how are the boys? Are they well?"

"Yes, Salka, they are both well." I don't think I sounded very convincing.

"Yossek, please, I must see them. Tell them to come out, please."

I went back to the barrack and asked the boys to come out so that their mother could see them, but by that time the patrol had come around, and all they were able to do was to wave to their mother from afar.

And so they did, every chance they got for the next week, unable to cry out, unable to express their grief.

At the end of the week, the Cremo trucks came to collect their prey. Like every society, Auschwitz practiced certain conventions, and one was to hand the condemned prisoners a quarter of a loaf of bread with a smear of marmalade to make them eager to get on the truck. When the selected were gathered for the last ride, they were handed the extra rations. They bit into the bread in a frenzy, their hunger taking precedence over any other emotion.

All but Davidek. He simply licked off the marmalade and held his portion of bread to his chest. When the truck revved its motor and started moving, he leaned to the side of the truck and pitched the bread to his brother Aamek.

The sweet face with the deep-set, beautiful dark eyes smiled and waved an everlasting good-bye to this cruel world of adults he could not comprehend.

Life in Camp A was a sort of preschool preparation for things to come. There was no official work schedule, but the block-eldests and their helpers made sure that our days were filled with cruelty. The workday consisted mainly of moving heavy rocks from one area to another and then back again, at break-neck speed under a barrage of insults, curses, and beatings.

Roll calls were the most dangerous. This was when the SS man on duty would strut in front of us, resplendent in his uniform, his whip neatly folded in his hand, looking for a victim so he could show off his skills. Invariably after being beaten to within an inch of their lives, the victims would be sent to the camp hospital—*Krankenbau* or Ka-Be—and would never be seen again.

Nothing in Auschwitz made sense. It seemed that every-thing there was designed to strip the inmates of any sense of rationality. The low numbers, the inmates who had survived this Gehenna long enough to become a part of the Auschwitz nomenclature, were devoid of normal, human feelings. To survive in Auschwitz meant to adopt the Auschwitz values and live by them, and the cheapest Auschwitz commodity was life itself.

Except for Davidek, our group from Blizyn was still intact. We toed the line, stayed out of trouble, and waited for events to unfold.

One morning, after the roll call, a list of needed crafts-men was read. As usual, mechanics were on top of the list. Bilke and I stepped out to join about two hundred men, all skilled in various crafts. Our numbers were noted, and we were separated from the others. Armed guards arrived with several capos and took charge of us. We were told that we were privileged because we were going to be transferred to Camp D.

I became Bilke's shadow. Things were breaking our way, as Boris, Bilke's sauna friend had predicted.

The group was formed into a marching column with the inevitable accompaniment of curses, threats, and blows. Then the capos tried to teach us marching skills so that we would look good as we entered the venerable gates of Camp D. It was a relatively short distance, but the guards and capos were determined to see us march as if on a parade. They drilled us for hours, *Eins, Zwei, Drei, Links, Eins, Zwei, Drei, Links*. Blows on the head reminded us to keep in step.

By late afternoon, our marching skills were deemed acceptable. The guards and the capos placed themselves all around the column to make sure everyone was in lockstep. The leading capo yelled, "Commando, march!" And in per-fect unison, we began marching. As we came closer to the entry gate of Camp D, I could hear strains of music and remembered the music I heard on the arrival ramp the first day. Then I saw other columns of prisoners converging on the entry gate from all directions—the other commandos returning from work. Our column was shunted aside to let them enter.

Awestruck, I watched one column after another cross the raised barrier at the point of entry. The prisoners looked like striped marionettes. Gaunt faces with fearful eyes, emaciated bodies in their striped uniforms from which their tin plates dangled on a string. As each column neared the raised barrier, the capo in charge screamed: *"Mutzen Ab!"* The entire column took off their caps in unbelievable unison, all against a backdrop of a clean, blue sky and beautiful classical music. An uninitiated onlooker would see it as a well-rehearsed pageant, if he didn't look closely at the eyes of the marchers.

Then came our turn. Spines stiffened, the adrenaline began to flow, and our column started marching: *Eins, Zwei, Drei, Links!* We knew that this was not the time to fumble or we might pay with our lives. The column now picked up the drumbeat of the music, and just before entry, the orders came as if from a Marine drill sergeant. *Kopf Hoch! Brust Raus! Kragen Runter! Links, Links, Links! Mutzen Ab!"*

As we passed the raised barrier, an SS man from the Camp D guardhouse counted us. He was accompanied by two youngsters, nine or ten years old, dressed in beautiful bellboy uniforms as if they were welcoming us to a fine hotel. I later learned that, for some unfathomable reason, these boys were referred to by the English word, "Pupils." They seemed perfectly at ease as if they had been there greeting new arrivals all of their lives.

As we kept marching in perfect unison, the music grew louder and more beautiful until we passed a raised platform where perhaps as many as fifty musicians were playing under the direction of a conductor who stood behind a lectern. One more bizarre detail in this most bizarre day.

We were ordered to halt, then to turn left on our heels and to keep marching in place. We now faced directly west into the last rays of the setting sun. It took a moment of squinting, but eventually my eyes focused on the scene in front of me. About a dozen corpses were sitting in a ditch that ran alongside the road. They were propped up to make them look alive, but each had his neck broken, and the heads were tilted to one side. All wore signs on their chests describing the "crime" they had committed for which they had been punished. The message was clear. We had to cooperate in our own degradation and destruction because to resist in any way was not to simply die, but to die a long, terrible, and tortured death.

We marched into Camp D along a "street," between two rows of barracks. At the side of each barrack was a lot where prisoners were beginning to line up for the evening roll call. The capos and the blockeldests were screaming at the prisoners and often striking them on the head. For the first time, I noticed the handsomely tailored uniforms and the healthy, ruddy faces of the capos and blockeldests. Instinctively, I knew that they were going to make the difference between living and dying.

Bilke and I were assigned to Block 28. After a terrible roll call, where the newcomers were singled out for abuse, we were given a piece of bread with marmalade. Following more screamed threats by our new master of life and death, the blockeldest, Pan Kowarski, we went to sleep on a three-tiered bunk, packed like sardines.

Just before I fell asleep, I remember being grateful that I still had my thinking process. The Nazis had taken everything from me, but they could not rob me of my soul. Deep down I mocked them more than ever. I knew that their days were numbered, whether or not I lived to see them defeated. The mere thought of their eventual downfall gave me the strength to face the next day.

Blockeldest Kowarski was a short, powerfully built, Polish Gentile with a shaggy mustache and a ruddy complexion. Like most blockeldests, he wore a zebra-striped uniform custom-tailored by some Jewish tailor for extra soup and bread. He reminded me of a butcher I knew in Radom. As a child, I had to pass this butcher's shop frequently because it was near the town's public library, and I always walked a little faster when I went by. He had such massive muscles and such a stern, mean look on his face that I dreaded being on the receiving end of his displeasure.

It was this kind of man I faced as my lord and master at roll call my first morning in Block 28.

The first order after the count off was for the newcomers to step out while everyone else scattered to join their assigned work units. A few of us, including Bilke and me, were selected to join a work unit under the command of a capo named Bolek. I had noticed Capo Bolek as he helped with the roll call. He was a dwarf with a mouth that spurted a continuous stream of anti-Semitic invective in cultured, refined Polish. He also carried a bamboo stick which he used to hit, poke, and prod people. He and Pan Kowarski were quartered together in a blocked-off section of the barrack. It was our bad luck to be chosen to work in his commando.

Capo Bolek, with the help of his stick, lined up the work unit—about fifty of us, mostly Hungarian Jews who had survived the selection on the arrival ramp. Once we were lined up, we started marching towards the gate, past the fifty-piece symphony orchestra. The music which had been so bizarre the day before now simply sounded hollow, accompanied as it was with Capo Bolek's shrill cries of "lazy, filthy, Jewish vermin!" Marching for half an hour or so, we reached our work area, where a private firm under contract to expand

Birkenau was building another subcamp to house more slaves for a nearby chemical plant. Several civilians, Swiss employees of the firm, awaited us, and the group was split up among them, each taking his workers in a different direction.

Bilke and I were assigned to move parts of preassembled huts closer to the building site. A rectangle had been marked off around the work area, and the two armed guards who had joined us at the camp gate placed themselves on high ground at either end of the rectangle, ready to shoot anyone who ventured beyond the line. Even so, escaping from a work commando was relatively easy since the guards could not keep track of all of us all the time. But it was nearly impossible to elude the constant patrols of the whole Auschwitz area, especially after an alarm had been sounded. And the alarm would sound quickly since there were three, sometimes four roll calls and countoffs, every day. We heard very early about the agonizing torture inflicted on captured escapees before they were hung in full view of the entire camp population. None of us thought of stepping out of that rectangle.

The day was awfully hot, the work exhausting, and Capo Bolek's stick and insults were unbearable. The only break came at noon, when several people were dispatched to bring us lunch. The food was brought in, and we lined up with our tin plates. One of Capo Bolek's adjutants doled out the soup with a ladle while the other helper handed each of us a slice of bread with a smear of margarine. We wolfed this down in an unbelievable frenzy. Then we watched Capo Bolek, his helpers, and the civilians eat their lunch of bread, eggs, and sausage, washed down with real coffee out of thermos bottles.

Bilke and I knew that no one could last long under these conditions so we decided to try to find Capo Janek, the contact Bilke's sauna friend had given us, as soon as we returned to camp.

As we worked through the interminable day, I watched our Hungarian fellow prisoners wilt. Bilke and I were at least hardened by years of cruelty in the ghettos and labor camps. These poor wretches had been normal human beings living in decent conditions as little as a month before their free fall into the Auschwitz abyss. When the pro-Nazi Hungarian government, under pressure from fascist elements in Hungary, consented to hand the Jews over to the Germans for annihilation, the "Final Solution" had been 80 percent accomplished. But to the Jewish-Hungarian victims, the fate of their German and Polish brethren remained an incomprehensible secret even this late in the war.

So now I watched the poor wretches go through the agony of adjustment to a life so appalling, so inconceivable that it defies description. Perhaps the hardest thing to see was their slow comprehension of the fate of their loved ones. That and the gentleness these people displayed, a gentleness that I had almost forgotten existed in the world. They were totally innocent of the way of the camps and hopelessly vulnerable.

I was then a tough and cynical seventeen years old.

When we got back to camp that evening, I found someone with a low number—someone who had been there a long time—and a yellow triangle and discreetly asked where I could find a capo named Janek.

"Be careful with such questions," the low number said. "Just mentioning Janek's name could get you in a lot of trouble."

"Thank you for the warning, friend."

"Forget about getting on Janek's commando, it's for old timers and people of influence," he said. "A new number like you will never get close to the boys who work in 'Canada.' Capo Janek's commando is the only work detail that has easy access to the people who sort the valuables. For one such as yourself to work there would be a miracle, and this is one place where miracles don't happen."

"Thank you for your valuable advice," I said, "but if my friend Bilke and I wished to locate Capo Janek, just to let him know of our existence, where might we find him?"

"If you persist in this foolishness, he is in block number eight, but be careful. Remember I warned you, just walking into his domain might cost you your lives."

The low number touched his head with his forefinger, then shrugged his shoulders and walked away.

After I told Bilke what the low number had said, we decided to hold off for a day to think it over. But the second day on the job with Capo Bolek resolved our uncertainty. If we were to stay there much longer, we were dead anyway.

The following day after work, we walked into Capo Janek's barrack and asked the block orderly where we could find him. He looked at the high numbers on our jackets and sniffed. Nothing in Birkenau was lower than a new arrival. He was about to give us a piece of his mind when a short, blond, young man appeared from behind a curtain that partitioned off the front of the barrack to create some privacy for those who were somebody in the Birkenau hierarchy.

"You are looking for Capo Janek?" the young man said.

Bilke and I nodded.

"Well, come on, you've found him." He motioned us to follow him behind the curtain.

Capo Janek lived in unbelievable luxury. He actually had furniture in his cubicle. There was a hard-backed chair that sat near a regular bed. In front of the bed was a high bench that served as a table. Above his bed were actual cabinets that I was sure held food. There were pots and pans, and clothing and shirts hanging from a rack, and several pairs of shoes and boots all shined up on a shelf. There was a wonderful smell of something being fried nearby.

Janek laughed at the shock on our faces. Then to confound us further, he took out a pack of cigarettes and nonchalantly offered us each one. He motioned for us to sit on his bed while he took the chair.

"First," he said, "be careful and keep your mouths shut. We don't want word of this to get out to anyone."

"Of course," Bilke said, "but how can we...?"

"You may not know this, but your friend Boris is a very powerful man in Birkenau."

"I had heard he works in ... Canada?" Bilke said.

Capo Janek laughed. "Ah, yes, the legendary land of milk and honey. You see, the sauna workers get to strip-search the new arrivals for valuables, and Boris is one of the few the Germans trust to keep a count on the gold coins."

We nodded. He didn't need to elaborate further. The picture was perfectly clear to a couple of old smugglers like us.

"Anyway," he said, "Boris asked me to help you, so I'll do what I can to transfer you to my commando. It may take some time. Meanwhile..."

He opened one of his cabinets and produced two beautiful apples. He gave one to each of us. "Wait until after lights out so no one can see when you eat them." He inquired of our barrack's number, bid us a courteous good-bye, and said that he'd be in touch. We left his barrack totally dazed. I thought of the old number's comment about miracles never happening in Birkenau.

That night I ate the apple, core and all, very slowly and very deliberately. Nothing in this world would ever taste so good again.

The meeting with Capo Janek gave Bilke and me a tremendous lift. The mere knowledge that there was a chance to get away from Capo Bolek made it easier to keep from wringing his neck when he poked us with his stick and threatened to send us all to the Cremo at the next selection. At times, however, I remember being very close to hitting him. Of course, any move against him would have been instantly fatal, but the insults, especially the anti-Jewish epithets that he hurled at us in a continuous stream all day long, were hard to take from someone I could crush without breaking into a sweat. Capo Janek's promise of better days to come kept me from committing suicide by attacking Capo Bolek.

The poor Hungarians were giving up by the dozen. Some had either lost or thrown away their tin plates. At first, it did not matter, since they couldn't stomach the camp soup. In fact, as they watched the rest of us eat the soup as if it was a gourmet treat, they sneered at us and called us garbage-eating pigs. But when real hunger set in, sooner for some, later for others, those without plates begged for a chance to take the soup in their wooden clogs. That was how far they had come. Men who had been respected professionals or craftsmen and had lived a near-normal life only a few weeks before were reduced to slurping soup out of a shoe, while Pan Kowarski, Capo Bolek, and their helpers taunted them and called them dirty Jewish animals, unworthy of living.

The deterioration process was relentless. First came the psychological shock when the meaning of the smoking chimneys and the fate of their loved ones sunk in, followed by long hours of hard labor, terrible beatings, and constant verbal denigration. But hunger was by far the greatest cause of despair. When they gave up hope, their eyes became vacant. Some would go on the electrified wire for a quick death. Most would lay down on the bunk for the night and expire without a whimper. Then there were the barrack selections, when those deemed unfit to work were selected and gassed.

So their ranks thinned quickly. But as soon as there was room in the barrack, another batch would arrive, and the process would start over again.

Bilke and I were able to endure this hell because of our experience and also because of our hope for improving our lot by joining Capo Janek's commando.

One day at the morning roll call, Pan Kowarski came to Bilke and me while counting and stopped. He looked at our faces then looked at our numbers. Our hearts sank—it wasn't safe to attract attention from the likes of Pan Kowarski. But all he did was ask if we were all right. We nodded, and he continued counting. That day when the soup was distributed at lunchtime, the foreman told Bilke and me to line up for another helping. Everyone else looked at us as if we had sold out to the enemy.

The following day, Pan Kowarski officially released Bilke and me from Capo Bolek's commando and told us to join Capo Janek's unit.

I didn't know quite what being in Capo Janek's unit meant, but I had a premonition that my chances for survival had gotten a significant boost.

When Bilke and I got to where Capo Janek's unit was forming, he barely acknowledged us. Then he gave the order to line up, and we fell in with about thirty other workers. Capo Janek marched us past the orchestra and through the gate with the usual head-high, collar-down, chest-out routine, but that day the music took on a new meaning. The drums rolled to a crescendo and gave way to the stringed instruments, plaintive and beautiful. Underneath the melody, the drums and cymbals kept the marching beat— *links, links, links*—and once again in my ordeal, I felt grateful to be alive. As we passed the gate on the way out, there was a new spring in my step, and Bilke looked just as elated because it was his friend that made it all possible. I noticed that guards didn't join us as we went through the gate, probably because our work area was considered secure.

We marched directly towards the four killing facilities, taking the same route we had taken when we entered Camp A on the day of our arrival. We passed the number four and five crematoria and came to a large meadow. In the middle of the meadow was an excavation with mounds of earth all around it. Nearby was a construction shack, where our column halted. Capo Janek unlocked the shack, peeked in to see if anything was disturbed, then gave orders to his two helpers to start the day's work. They split the commando into two groups. One stayed by the shack and the other, including Bilke and I, lined up again and marched a short distance to the railroad tracks between crematoria number two and three.

There were two rail lines that went as far back as the arched gates of the entry building. Capo Janek led us to a freight car that rested against a stanchion at the end of the tracks some yards past the crematoria. He broke the seal on the door and opened it wide. Inside the car was a load of cement bags, as well as other building materials. All of us

lined up and began to unload. I asked one of my coworkers
what the materials were for, and he said, "for a swimming
pool." I laughed.

Bilke and I immediately noticed the difference in being
under Capo Janek's command. Capo Janek never yelled or
ridiculed anybody, and the workers of his commando didn't
seem afraid of him. Also, although he was Polish and Gentile, he treated the Poles and the Jews on his commando
alike. There was a healthier look and a more relaxed manner to his charges. Everyone did his share, and there was no
shirking, as there was on Capo Bolek's commando. I noticed
that prisoners who ran errands between the crematoria occasionally stopped to chat with some of the workers from our
group. I asked a fellow near me if these prisoners were from
the dreaded *Sonderkommando*, and he nodded.

It was astonishing. On the one hand, it was a beautiful
summer day with a clear blue sky and birch trees in full
bloom all around us, and I was working in almost-civilized
conditions. On the other hand, the air was sweet and clear
because the crematoria chimneys had not yet smoked that
day. This was where the crime of genocide was being committed every day, and I was in the belly of the beast.

And to add to the sense of the bizarre, it seemed that we
really were building a swimming pool.

We broke for lunch and returned to the shack where soup
and bread were being distributed. I noticed that some of the
fellows had no interest in the soup, instead they took the
bread and margarine, went off by themselves, and
unwrapped parcels of extra food they had brought with them.
I also noticed that no one carried the usual tin plate. Instead
they all used a military version of a mess kit, which we
called *menashka*.

And then Bilke and I discovered what a gift his friend Boris had given us. Capo Janek motioned to us to help ourselves to the extra soup. For the first time since we came to Auschwitz, we were able to eat to our heart's content.

While we were eating, I saw several trucks full of SS guards and prisoners coming down the road alongside the tracks. A van marked with the Red Cross trailed behind them, with a small staff car with several SS officers behind that. The convoy stopped at the unloading ramp. When we returned to work, I saw guards strung out on both sides of the tracks, most of them with baying dogs straining at their leashes. There were also prisoners from Canada on the ramp. A transport was about to arrive, and the Auschwitz assembly line of death was ready to go into action.

Soon we heard the whistle of the approaching train. I recalled waiting impatiently at the railroad station in Pionki, when my father was due to arrive for a summer weekend with the family. The whistle of the locomotive then was a happy sound, a harbinger of good times. Now...

When the whistle sounded one of my coworkers, a Gentile Polish boy said, "Here comes another batch of the chosen people."

Another said, "Yeah, tomorrow we eat Hungarian salami."

These comments were made without malice. Just statements of fact, about everyday life at Birkenau.

A few minutes later, the train lurched to a stop. The doors were opened and a sea of humanity flooded the ramp. At first there was a lot of commotion, but after a few warnings from the experienced SS on the ramp, everyone followed orders. The new arrivals were sorted into several columns. First came the survivors, those destined for work—one column of men and one of women. They were marched to the sauna building to undergo the camp initiation. When they came out the other side, an hour or so later, they had been transformed swiftly and efficiently into a subhuman species so dazed by the experience that they could barely recognize each other. All their hair was gone, and they wore striped suits that were either too long or too short and a pair of wooden clogs that made it almost impossible to walk. A round striped cap completed the look.

Those were the lucky ones. The rest were lined up for the short walk into oblivion. As they passed, they looked at us with eyes full of fear, and we looked away. Capo Janek had warned us not to make any remarks, especially not the finger across the throat sign.

I saw it all that first day. Well-dressed women in high heels cuddling infants. Others pushing beautiful baby carriages with nickel-plated hardware that reflected back the golden rays of the afternoon sun. Grandmothers often held several screaming children, because the Canada boys on the ramp told the mothers to hand their children to the elderly, thereby saving some young mothers for slave labor. I saw older men of all walks of life. Some were dressed like burghers in well-fitting suits with polished shoes. A few still carried briefcases. Many older men wore the traditional Jewish garb. Some walked with open prayer books, quietly beseeching God not to abandon them. Then came the "Red Cross" van loaded with people who were too sick to walk. One of the other workers told me the red cross painted on the van was a sham to quell the terrible fears of the people and to keep them docile to the last minute.

That last minute came quickly. All of these people were herded into the "shower room," and the airtight doors closed behind them. Then Zyklon B gas was introduced through special vents. Within one half hour, the doors were opened, the poisoned air extracted by a ventilation system, and the *Sonderkommando* began the grisly task of the disposal of the bodies. The stack of crematorium number two began to smoke, and the air filled with the stench of burning flesh.

As I watched this scene, my mouth became completely dry. I felt as I did the day Jacob told me about the meaning of Treblinka where my parents and my sister Bluma perished under the same circumstances. Once again, I wished desperately that I had gone with them. I noticed that the few Jewish workers in our commando moved their lips in prayer saying Kaddish (the Hebrew prayer for the dead). Bilke and I joined them.

At that moment, I felt that I had peeked over the mountain of life. I felt that I belonged more with the dead than with the living. At the age of seventeen, I had seen it all. The sorting commando of the Canada group, who were present on the ramp, loaded the trucks with the people's luggage, all carefully marked to prevent loss. All the worldly possessions brought by the unfortunate people that day went into the Canada sorting compound, including doubtless the Hungarian sausages that would find their way into my fellow-workers *menashkas* in a short time.

That afternoon the train brought about four thousand people into Auschwitz. By the time Capo Janek blew the whistle for us to line up and go back to camp, no trace remained of the three thousand or so who entered the gate of crematorium number two. No trace, except the billows of smoke that rose from the chimney.

I was barely aware of the march back. Nothing made sense anymore, not even my struggle to survive in order to bear witness. What I saw on that day, what I knew about the almost total extermination of European Jewry, had to be ordained by forces stronger than the SS troopers present on the ramp. This relentless subhuman policy of wholesale murder of innocent men, women, and children went beyond reason, and the most shocking aspect of it all was the very ordinariness with which it was treated by all who were involved. Three thousand men, women, and children driven into a sealed underground chamber, killed in a barbaric fashion, sent up in smoke, and an hour later everything was back to normal. It was like the story I remembered from my childhood of the fire-breathing dragon who went back to sleep each time he consumed his prey.

After lights out, I closed my eyes, but the comments of my fellow workers about the chosen people and Hungarian salami reverberated in my mind. I kept thinking of an old and oft-repeated Russian proverb: "You will either get used to it or perish."

Finally, I went to the back of the barrack where they kept the slop pail for the night. The back door was open, and a few prisoners were outside getting a bit of fresh air. I joined them. The night sky was lit up by fires from crematoria number four and five. A couple of transports had evidently arrived that evening and their bodies were being burned in open pits—numbers four and five had broken down from overuse. We were close enough to hear the fires crackling and feel the added heat on an already hot night. The stench was dreadful. The group around me were Gentile Poles and Russians, and here again the conversation was about the chosen people and the riches brought in by the Jews who were being turned into ashes in front of our eyes. I joined the group, but I kept silent.

Then another man came out, a Jewish-Hungarian survivor from the recent transports. He sniffed. In a mixture of
Yiddish and German, he asked, "What are the fires?"

The answer was a deadly silence.

"No, please," he said. There was a hint of panic in his
voice. "I am new here. What are they burning?"

Finally, one of the Russian boys pointed to the fires. "Do
you think they are frying potatoes for tomorrow's lunch, you
idiot? They are burning Jews! What do you think this camp
is for?"

The Hungarian looked at us, then at the fires. I could see
the horrible truth sinking in. Then he went over to a pole
in the barrack vestibule and began smashing his head against
it, wailing in Hebrew, "God, why have you forsaken us?" I
couldn't bear the blood flowing freely from his head and went
to restrain him.

He slipped out of my grasp and went straight for the electrified barbed wire.

There was a hiss, and his body fell back blackened and
motionless. Everyone returned to his bunk in silence.

The next day he was only one of the dozen or so who died
each night. He was counted as present by the scribe in the
morning roll call then simply deducted from the total. After
all, when you are under Germans, *Ordnung muss sein!*—
order must prevail.

The second day on the job with Capo Janek, I began learning the power structure in Auschwitz/Birkenau. At the pin-

nacle were the prisoners who were involved with the con-
fiscation of goods brought in by the Jewish victims—the
Canada workers. The transports arriving almost daily from
western Europe and Germany were particularly lucrative.
Those in charge of the Final Solution didn't want to attract
undue attention or protest from the local populations in
western Europe. So the death-train journeys there were still
called "deportations" as if they were merely a change of
address, and the Jews boarding those trains were allowed to
take all their possessions with them. Passengers on death-
trains from the west also traveled in reasonably good condition not to attract undue attention.

It was quite common for the Canada sorters to find
thousands of dollars or pound sterling in the purses of some
individuals. There was such an abundance of gold coins
that they were kept in buckets until there was time to sort
and count them for shipment to Germany. Naturally corruption was rampant in spite of the threat of torture, then
death by public hanging. Even high echelon SS officers
pocketed valuables and dispensed favors to prisoners in
exchange for gold. If you knew the right people, you could
buy almost anything in Camp D between the evening roll
call and lights out.

Capo Janek's commando turned out to be in charge of
building water reservoirs. They were made of concrete, six
feet deep, twelve feet wide, and about thirty feet long. The
first one had been built on the arrival ramp next to the SS
shack, and my commando was building several more, all
very close to the killing facilities. We called them swimming pools, because we were convinced that they were
meant to be mistaken for swimming pools by incoming
victims.

Rumor was that Capo Janek's commando would next be in charge of building a roof over the arrival ramp so that it looked like a normal railroad stop, another way to keep people calm as they marched to the gas chambers.

Because Capo Janek's commando worked so close to the sauna and the crematoria, his men were able to tap into the black market. Also a lot of trading went on between Capo Janek's workers and the members of the *Sonderkommando*. There was a difference between the Canada and *Sonderkommando* duties. The Canada workers were charged with "greeting" the new arrivals on the ramp and taking possession of their baggage. They also staffed the sauna and processed the new arrivals destined for slave labor. The *Sonderkommando*'s duties were to deal with the people destined for annihilation. To reduce the victims intense anxiety, they accompanied the victims to the gas chamber, made sure they were undressed, clipped the hair of the women, then withdrew just before the doors closed and the gas pellets were introduced. After waiting for the doors to reopen and the air in the gas chamber to be exhausted by giant fans, they began the grisly job of first removing the gold teeth and then burning the bodies.

Technically, they were confined to their quarters within the crematoria's electrified double-fence enclosure and were not permitted to communicate with any outsiders. But because of the job they had, *Sonderkommando* workers were treated with fear by their fellow prisoners and respect by their German bosses. This respect made it possible for them to move relatively freely between the two facilities. Since part of their job was to strip the victims before they entered the gas chambers, they, too, had access to the riches flowing through Birkenau.

Bilke and I began to take advantage of our privileged position when a member of the *Sonderkommando* approached and asked us to bring him some alcohol in exchange for food and gold. We told him to give us a few days and proceeded to ask discreetly about the alcohol trade. We found that the only thing Jews didn't, as a rule, take along on their last journey was any kind of alcoholic beverage, and there was nothing the *Sonderkommando* needed more. They were willing to risk their lives for any liquid with an alcoholic content to dull their senses and enable them to keep their sanity.

At the other end of the alcohol-for-food pipeline were fifty prisoners who worked in a large warehouse where all kinds of badly damaged aircraft were brought in to be salvaged. Because the Germans had very little gasoline, some of their planes were flying on refined grain alcohol, which meant the petrol still in their tanks was drinkable and very intoxicating. Since the members of Capo Janek's commando had access to both the *Sonderkommando* and the aircraft commando workers, we became the middlemen. The mess kit was the key to this highly sophisticated trade. A mess kit full of refined fuel cost one gold coin and fetched two or more coins plus some food when sold to a member of the *Sonderkommando*.

When Bilke and I found this out, we asked Capo Janek to put us in touch with Boris. The next day, Capo Janek handed us each two small Russian gold coins and told us that Boris would come one day soon to see us while at work. That evening after roll call, we bought two mess kits full of alcohol and the following day exchanged them for several gold coins plus two mess kits full of cheese, canned fish, and, yes, Hungarian salami. This was our first business transaction in the shadow of crematoria two and three. In the evening when we returned to Camp D, we bought more alcohol-fuel and used the profit to buy more food.

As if by magic, Pan Kowarski and his barrack helpers began to treat us kindly. We no longer had to stand on line when the soup was distributed, which was the ultimate mark of affluence. Boris came to see us several times while we were at work, and with each visit he brought a few gold coins, which we distributed strategically, mainly to Pan Kowarski and his cohorts. Daily we brought food in our mess kits and gave some to the starving unfortunates. And we ate enough to rebuild our own strength. With each bite of food, I felt more vigor return.

After a while, we learned of an active underground operating in the shadows of the crematoria. Certain German guards were bribed to smuggle arms and dynamite to the members of the *Sonderkommando*.

Some of the most privileged low numbers were involved, Jews and Poles alike. It was said that several Jewish girls were smuggling dynamite to the *Sonderkommando* from their workplace. We heard rumors about an impending mass breakout, and just hearing such rumors was dangerous because it meant that the Germans were on alert.

The punishments for conspiracy were draconian and the successes limited—only a handful of people escaped in the entire history of Auschwitz. But the war's end was approaching and an Allied victory was clearly in sight. More and more people on the outside were now willing to cooperate in plots against the Nazis, and on the inside, fear of retaliation after the war made it harder for the Germans to recruit spies within the ranks of prisoners.

And so my life in Auschwitz settled once again into a routine of smuggling, risking my life every minute of the day,
to stay alive. There was an internal security group in
Auschwitz charged with the detection of conspiracies and
prevention of theft and corruption—almost like an internal
Gestapo. This organization was mostly staffed with German
nationals, prisoners slated to be paroled. They were much
feared even by the privileged prisoners because every prisoner, no matter how privileged, was subject to their surprise
searches and interrogations. They constantly roamed the
camp in search of victims, and the fact that our commando
worked in close proximity to Canada and the crematoria
made us a special target. Bilke and I were frisked by them
on a number of occasions, and once Bilke had to swallow several gold coins when he saw them approach.

On certain days, Bilke and I were able to bribe our way
into maintenance crews of plumbers, electricians, and
roofers who worked in the women's compounds. On such a
day, I met Salka Birenbaum. When she saw me, she threw
her arms around me.

"Yossek, you are still alive, thank God!"

"Yes, Salka, I am well. A friend of Bilke's managed to get
us on a good commando."

"And Aamek, he is still well?"

"He is. I help him when I can."

"Thank you, Yossek. And Davidek, can you help him, too?"

"Davidek? Salka, please, Davidek is gone."

"No, no, no! He is in the Ka-Be. Some of the low numbers here have told me they would never gas one so young and beautiful as he. Please, Yossek, this good position you have, can you use it to get into the Ka-Be and help him?"

What was I to say? I knew Davidek was gone, he had definitely been gassed—I saw so many youngsters, so many infants marched to the gas chamber every day. And even if he were sent to the Ka-Be, I knew that most of the patients who went in there were swiftly dispatched with an overdose of phenobarbital. I was past the stage of delusions.

But Salka could not accept Davidek's death, and how could I rob her of her illusions? I watched her tortured face.

"I can't get into the Ka-Be myself," I said at last, "but I will ask friends, and if I hear anything of him, I will let you know."

Later she learned the times Capo Janek's commando passed near the fence of her camp on the way to work and back. From then on, she would stand there, nearly every day, and call out, "Yossek, have you seen Davidek?"

On another occasion I went to work for a day to the FKL, *Frauen Konzentrazions Lager*, an entire women's complex located on the other side of the arrival ramp, directly across from Camp D. While I was walking along the road inside the compound, someone called my name. I spun around to see who it was who knew me in that nether world, and I saw the smiling, beautiful face of Basia Greenshpan, my friend and fellow student from Miss Soboll's underground school. She was on crutches and had a cast on one of her legs—a bizarre sight in that setting. I almost ran up to embrace her, but I couldn't attract the capo's attention.

Later that day, she was able to come over to where we were repairing an inner fence, and she told me how she came to be wearing a cast. She had tripped and fallen on the wooden clogs she was given on the day of her arrival, but she managed to limp into the barrack after her injury. She was subsequently sent to the Ka-Be where a German doctor set her broken bone and sent her back to camp. Miraculously, this doctor thought she was too young and beautiful for the usual injection of phenobarbital.

On another day, when a train on the ramp was unloading its cargo of emaciated survivors of the Lodz ghetto, we saw the SS pull aside an elderly white-haired man. They seemed to fuss over him as if he were someone famous. Later, I was told by one of the *Sonderkommandos* that the man who attracted the attention of the killers was Chaim Rumkowski, the head of the Lodz ghetto. The Germans called him the King of the Jews.

For more than four years, he held absolute power over the Lodz Jews and cooperated with the Germans as much as possible, in the belief that hard work on behalf of the German war machine would save the lives of his people. The result was slow starvation of the ghetto inhabitants, and when time ran out, a fast ride to the ovens in Birkenau. The entire transport was gassed that day, including Mr. Rumkowski. But the Germans did give him the courtesy of individual attention as they walked him into the gas chamber chatting and talking amiably.

Each Sunday after morning roll call, all inmates were ordered to assemble at the entry gate in a semicircle, where there was a row of gallows. Then several unfortunates were brought out, visibly tortured and broken wearing signs telling of the "crimes" they had committed. Each was brought to the gallows and unceremoniously hanged by the neck. The others waited their turn until the previous body stopped twitching. When the ritual was finished, the bodies were placed in a nearby ditch and propped up for all to see as they passed the gate to and from work. In cool weather they would be there for days.

Afterwards the musicians took their places for the Sunday concert. If the hangings finished early, the musicians had to wait until the service at the town church was over, because a lot of the SS and their families who were quartered in town attended. Many German civilians would also drive to the camp after church to enjoy classical music played by some of the best musicians in Europe.

I often wondered about the sermons those Germans listened to just before they came to the Sunday concert at the local human slaughterhouse. Surely the minister had to know what Auschwitz was for. How did he rationalize the deeds of his parishioners? Did he shake their bloody hands and wish them Godspeed and success in their endeavors?

The worst days on Capo Janek's commando were the days when trucks arrived from nearby satellite camps bringing the selected victims who were no longer fit for work. These victims knew exactly what awaited them and fought against their fate with all the strength they had left. The crematoria SS crews were not allowed to waste bullets on this human "flotsam." *Schade Kugel*, save bullets, was the standing order. So they had to physically round them up and force them into the gas chamber. Sometimes it took hours. The screams were heart wrenching, even to the most hardened of us.

Sometimes special passenger trains arrived, carrying western Jews of aristocratic families who still had friends in high places in the Nazi hierarchy. For these people the Nazis had devised an ingenious plan. Such people weren't killed outright but were usually confined in holdover places, like the ghettos in the east or the model camp at Theresienstadt. They were encouraged to write to their friends of their whereabouts, which perpetuated the legend that "deportation" was just a change of address. After these people had contributed their part to the legend, they were loaded on passenger trains and brought in comfort to the gas chambers.

On one memorable day, an elegant train consisting mostly of Pullman cars pulled into the Birkenau siding. Several vans with the Red Cross markings and many more guards than usual were there to meet it, but the barking dogs were gone. When the doors opened, German soldiers dressed in World War I uniforms emerged along with their elegantly dressed families. Most of the soldiers had the German Iron Cross dangling from their necks and a lot were wheelchair-bound.

We watched in stupefied horror as the SS killers on the ramp clicked their heels, saluted, then reverently loaded them into the vans, drove them to the crematorium gate, and ushered them in with the same show of respect. After the doors were sealed, the well-known command—"Hans, let them have something to eat"—was given and the Zyklon B pellets dropped.

On one unusually clear, crisp day, a transport of Jews arrived from Budapest. It was the first arrival that day and the air was still clear of the foul smell. As the people tumbled out of the boxcars, I could see that there was a larger percentage of the Orthodox among them than usual. Because they had beards that made them look older, a larger than usual number were selected to die. As they passed on their way to the crematorium, they stopped no more than a few feet from us because of a holdup at the gate. For the first time, I came face to face with the victims.

An elderly man who had been praying from an open book stopped and looked at me closely. "You are a Jew," he said in Yiddish.

I nodded.

"Tell me, what is the meaning of the tall chimneys? What will happen to us?"

Mindful of Capo Janek's order, I remained silent.

"My child," he said, "I can see that you are not allowed to talk to us, but I know you understand me. Just nod your head. Are we going *Al Kiddush Hashem*?"

I could no longer restrain myself and said in Yiddish, "Rabbi, this would be a good time for the Messiah to come."

He didn't seem startled and accepted my answer as a confirmation of his fears. He reopened the book and continued his prayers. As the column started moving, he turned and said, "The Messiah will come when no one will need Him."

Days turned into weeks and weeks into months. October 1944 brought the first chilly winds of fall. The days were clear, and Allied reconnaissance planes were over our heads almost every day. We cheered them openly and prayed that they would come down and blow the whole camp to kingdom come. We would all welcome such a death, if it would also punish our tormentors and at least temporarily stop the genocide.

Soon there were occasional night attacks on the industrial targets nearby, and the explosions were the sweetest music I ever heard. God, how we loved to watch the SS supermen scramble for protection in mortal fear of the bombs. Finally, after so many years of suffering, we had lived to see the day when we could feel superior to them. It didn't matter that they could still kill us at will and often did, we knew, and they knew, that their days of glory were ending. And that knowledge was sweet, and it stiffened our spines.

But the trains still kept coming. The Germans stuck to their relentless quest to make Europe free of Jews, as if possessed, in spite of their deteriorating military position.

One day while at work we heard shooting near us. Very quickly the camp alarm sounded, and many helmeted, battle-ready SS soldiers appeared all around us armed with submachine guns and hand grenades. We were ordered to hit the dirt and we did. We then heard several explosions coming from numbers four and five crematoria and a loud "Hurrah" from behind the number two facility. The rumors that the *Sonderkommando* boys were going to make a run for freedom had finally come true. I spent the next two hours or so with my face in the dirt, listening to the shooting and screaming. When we were finally permitted to rise, I saw that the chimney of number four was gone, and we saw several bodies of SS men and many dead prisoners in striped clothing laying in the distance.

For the next few weeks, we were forced to watch the daily public hangings of the people accused of helping in the conspiracy. The full fury of the Third Reich was unleashed on the camp population in the most gruesome acts of vengeance. Every day there were new revelations of important prisoners who were involved in the uprising. The methods used to obtain confessions under torture were the most brutal ever devised. Sooner or later, everyone cracked and the hangmen were constantly busy. In addition, the SS kept bringing in escapees from the *Sonderkommando* who were captured in the surrounding countryside.

Capo Janek's commando was assigned two guards after the uprising. Their orders were to watch us every minute of the day. The crematoria kept working, but on a much reduced level and with a smaller crew.

Bilke and I held our own. Our bodies were in good physical shape, and we still had no problem obtaining extra food, even though contact with the *Sonderkommando* was sporadic. We still saw Boris on occasion, too. I had expected him to be implicated in the breakout because I knew that he was actively involved. He was the source of some of the gold used to bribe the Germans to obtain weapons and dynamite. He later told us that he survived by bribing the very SS interrogators who conducted the investigation.

By the middle of October, we noticed a marked reduction in the trains coming in and a considerable increase in outgoing traffic. Daily, trains were loaded with prisoners and sent to destinations all over Germany. The Russians had launched a powerful offensive on the southern front that brought them dangerously close to Auschwitz. The end was in sight, but our anxiety about survival grew. The weather turned nasty, and cold winds began to blow. In the middle of November, Capo Janek informed us that his commando was to be disbanded, which meant that Bilke and I would be picked for the next transport out.

Cleanup crews that had been left behind in camps in Poland, such as Blizyn, were now coming into Auschwitz after their jobs had been completed. Among these crews were former camp orderlies and other assorted big shots who no longer had any clout in the new Birkenau setting. Some of these people were being fingered as collaborators when they encountered those whom they had mistreated.

More often than not, the man who brought them to justice was Pincus, the Jewish blockeldest of barrack number nineteen. Pincus was a man in his late thirties, about five feet six, stocky, and powerfully built. His face was ruddy, and when he talked, his voice was coarse and gravelly. He had been a butcher in Lodz and was so strong, it was said he could break a man's neck with one blow. He was the most powerful, the most-feared Jewish blockeldest in Birkenau. He was also a kind of Robin Hood helping Jewish victims in other barracks run by Gentiles like Pan Kowarski by threatening to retaliate against Polish Gentile prisoners.

On several occasions, Bilke and I witnessed kangaroo trials held in Block 19 presided over by Pincus. When a man was accused of wrongdoing or collaboration, Pincus would look around the barrack and ask if there was anyone present that would defend him. If not, Pincus would mete out swift and immediate justice accompanied by derisive comments such as, "So you forgot you are a Jew. I am here to remind you." In a sordid way, we all applauded these denunciations and the dispensation of kangaroo justice. We couldn't get back at our real tormentors, but it was consoling to see the collaborators get it.

It was my luck to be present one evening in Pincus's barrack when several such collaborators were brought in to face the Pincus court. One of them was Sol Mincberg, who was denounced as the former head of the Blizyn camp. Bilke and I immediately vouched for Sol's credentials. Our vehement pleading plus several gold coins helped get him off. We then took him to our barrack, gave him something to eat, and listened to his report about the fifty men left behind in Blizyn.

All fifty eventually found out about the underground canal and the escape route that Bilke and I worked many hours to prepare. But they faced the same problem we did—they had no place to run to. So they decided to wait until the Russians started their next offensive and crossed the Vistula River. Their plan was to escape as soon as the artillery barrages started. The Russians were known for their tremendous artillery barrages before their troops jumped off.

When the camp work was nearing the end and almost all equipment had been dismantled and shipped to Germany, Engineer Baum with about twenty men disappeared from the camp when the rest, including Sol, were out at the railroad station loading the last freight cars. As soon as the escape was noted by the Germans, the rest of them were put on a truck and brought to Auschwitz.

When we took Sol back to his barrack, we assured him of our help as long as we remained in Birkenau, but we told him that the camp was being evacuated, and we may get shipped out in a matter of days.

Several days later, Pan Kowarski told Bilke and me that he had assigned us to what he knew was a "good" camp, and we were to leave that day.

On the way out of camp, we underwent the same sauna ritual that we did on the way in, but this time we were ready for it, and it was less painful. It also gave us a chance to see Boris for the last time. When we came out on the "clean" side, stark naked in the November cold, we lined up to receive new clothing. Boris had prepared good overcoats with fur collars for each of us. He also managed to tell us to check the linings of the coats where he had inserted a few gold coins.

We said a tearful good-bye to Boris. He did more than anyone else I encountered on my long journey to help me survive. I never even learned his family name.

For the last time we marched to the infamous Birkenau ramp. One of the crematoria chimneys was still smoking, but I could tell it wasn't working at full capacity. The only thought in my head that day was whether I would ever be able to reveal to the world the things I witnessed there.

That, and whether anyone would believe it.

We boarded the familiar freight car with the inevitable slop pail. The door was shut and bolted from the outside. The familiar whistle blew, and I was off to the final part of my odyssey.

CHAPTER 7

LIEBEROSE AND TRANSIT

We rode the train from Auschwitz for about twenty-four hours before it eased to a halt. The doors of the freight cars opened onto a normal railroad station. It was early morning and cold. There was snow on the ground. The only people in sight were our guards and several SS officers who were evidently our new patrons of life and death. There was an abundance of blue-white signs on the station that bore the name "Lieberose."

The eight hundred or so prisoners in the transport were lined up in marching order, and we set out for our new home. The march took us through the main street of the village. For the first time in a years, I was able to see a tranquil, normal place, and my eyes feasted on the scene. It seemed that the war hadn't touched this lovely, sleeping village full of neat homes, tall, partly snow-covered pine trees, and sharp, clean, fresh air. The time was around Christmas, and most of the homes were decorated for the holiday. We were in a winter wonderland, and the spirit of goodwill which I always associated with Christmas sent my hopes soaring. In those days, it didn't take much to set my hopes soaring.

After marching for about an hour beyond the village, we came to a clearing in a pine forest. The familiar guard towers came into view, then the electrified barbed wire, the barracks, the stench of death, all the familiar signs of my life. Then we passed the gate and could see the prisoners, and whatever hopes I may have had died. They were in a terrible state. The prisoners were emaciated, walking corpses with bulging eyes and hollow cheeks. Their look was familiar to veterans like Bilke and me. It was the look of people who had lost the will to live.

When we were ensconced in a barrack and had a chance to talk to the camp inhabitants, our worst fears were confirmed. Camp Lieberose had once been a model concentration camp where mostly German nationals were interned for short periods for minor offenses. The camp was administered by German criminals taken from jails where they were serving long sentences and pressed into service by the SS. Now, the prisoners for whom the camp was built were long gone, "freed" and sent to the meat grinder on the Russian front. At this time, the camp was used as a way station for prisoners evacuated from the threatened eastern regions.

Lieberose was clean, its barracks weren't crowded, and the sanitation facilities were good. The camp routine was the same as in Auschwitz, with twice daily roll calls and the barrackeldest and his helpers distributed the food after each roll call. But because Lieberose was just a holding center, there was no work, no industry, no production on site. Most important, there was no chance to "organize" extra food beyond the daily ration of two slices of bread and a quart of watery turnip soup.

Occasionally, healthier-looking prisoners would be chosen after the morning roll call, for a minor work detail. Local merchants sometimes requested help with heavy work such as unloading coal or lumber. Often groups of prisoners were taken to nearby towns to clear up the rubble after air bombardments. But the main purpose of the camp was to keep the prisoners penned until they could be shipped to anyone in need of slave labor.

Bilke and I were still very much dependent on each other. Each of us had several gold coins that we had recovered from under the lining of the winter coats Boris gave us, but we didn't dare utter a word about them to anyone until we had a chance to acquaint ourselves with the power structure of the camp and find a likely green triangle in charge who might be open to taking a bribe in exchange for food. We had to be extremely careful whom we chose, since the green triangles had all the power. They might simply beat us and demand the gold, or take the gold and give nothing in return.

In the meantime, and for the first time since we started working for Capo Janek, food intake became the main focus of our lives. Around us were prisoners who had been men of substance, power and wealth, with the finest family and intellectual backgrounds. Hunger now reduced them to beggarly wretches. Some would gobble the food as quickly as they could stuff it in their mouths. Others went off to a corner and ate slowly and deliberately, delighting in each morsel as if it were a feast. Still others would bite off a piece of the bread and wrap the rest for later. Sometimes there were cries in the middle of the night as someone tried to steal these hoarded portions.

But most managed to remain human, even in the midst of starvation. On Sundays, we divided into groups of six, and each group was given a two-pound loaf of bread. The first of the six on line was given the bread and the responsibility to divide it equally. Each group would then go off to a bunk for the ritual of the cutting. Careful measurements were made, makeshift scales were used, the six pieces were carefully cut and weighed, then lots were drawn for each piece. The ritual was terribly demeaning, but at the same time, it was miraculously civilized.

The soup was cooked in large cauldrons in the camp kitchen, then transferred into smaller kettles for distribution to various barracks. It was a privilege to be dispatched to fetch the soup kettles because those who brought the soup were entitled to the leftovers. After the soup was distributed, they would tilt the empty kettles and scrape every bit they could with spoons. They then turned the kettles over to others who were so desperately hungry that they stuck their heads deep into the kettles and licked them clean before finally washing them and taking them back to the kitchen. Licking the kettle was considered to be the final act of humiliation. The Germans delighted in watching prisoners do it and often snapped pictures of the act. They probably sent the pictures home as proof that their charges in the camps were *Untermenschen* and deserved their fate.

After three weeks of these conditions, Bilke and I knew that we had to act soon. Bilke's eyes became wide with the desperate, vacant look of the starving, and his body began to shrink. I started to check my feet daily to see if there was any swelling at the ankles, the telltale mark of the first stage of starvation.

Finally, we picked one of the green triangles named Conrad, the blockeldest of a neighboring barrack. He fit the criteria we'd set for someone likely to respond to a bribe. First, he treated his charges with a modicum of humaneness. Second, he distributed the leftover soup in a fair way giving extra soup to different people each day. Third, he had a soft look and seemed accessible.

I was the one to make the approach because I spoke German well. But just in case, we hid our treasure in several different places, and neither of us knew where the other had chosen. That way, if one us was caught and tortured, he would not be able to reveal the other's hiding places.

Finally, I took my life in my hands and approached blockeldest Conrad. "Sir, if you please, might I have a moment of your time?"

It was such a simple request. Yet I was so filled with a fear that I was almost unable to make myself understood. I was about to own up to the fact that I had gold, which put me at the mercy of the most brutal element in the camp.

Our choice proved justified. Conrad didn't become abusive. He merely said, "What do you have to say to me?"

"I have something of value, which I would like to show you in the privacy of your room."

He stared at me for a long moment, then said, "This evening, before lights out."

That evening I stood in front of the door to the small room of the barrack from which Conrad ruled over the three hundred prisoners in his domain. I clutched a small Russian gold piece in my sweaty hand. Bilke waited outside for the results. I knocked. Conrad ushered me in.

I presented him with the gold piece. "What is this worth to you, Sir?"

He looked it over carefully, then excused himself, and stepped out of the room. Presently he returned.

"This gold piece, this single gold piece, is worth one slice of bread and one portion of soup. If there are other gold pieces, they may be worth substantially more. Who knows?"

"Sir, might I please have an additional portion of bread and soup?"

"You are hardly in a position to be greedy."

"No sir, but this is for my partner. He is waiting outside the door."

Conrad held up the gold piece. "And would your partner have more of these?"

"He might. I don't know."

Conrad smiled and had me bring in Bilke. Then he gave each of us a slice of bread and about a quart of soup.

For the next ten days Bilke and I exhausted our supply of gold in return for this daily bit of food. It didn't begin to quench the terrible hunger in our bellies, but we knew that in the long run it could make the difference between life and death.

Conditions in the camp were turning from bad to worse. Every morning, droves of bodies were removed from the bunks and placed in front of the barrack before roll call. For easier identification, their numbers were written on their backs in large letters. Then a truck came and took the bodies to the crematorium at Oranienburg. I looked at the daily supply of dead and wondered when my turn would come.

I developed sores on the back of my neck, and they became infected. There was no question of obtaining medical help—there was a building in the camp with a big sign *Lazaret* (hospital), but not one of the people who went in there came out alive. So one day Bilke borrowed a sharp knife from the barrack orderly, disinfected it over an open flame, cut my sores open, and carefully squeezed the pus out. The "operation" was so painful, and I fainted several times. When he was done, Bilke tore a piece of a shirt from one of the deceased and used it for a bandage. Miraculously, the boils never came back.

Whenever there was a chance to go out of camp on a work detail, Bilke and I always volunteered because sometimes we got extra food. One day we were taken to the railroad station to unload bags of horse-meal. It was a mixture of oats, grain, and straw. Inevitably some of it got spilled, and some prisoners began to eat it. I remember putting some of it in my mouth. I chewed it, but I couldn't swallow. Still, I remember thinking how lucky the horses were to eat such good food.

After about six weeks in Lieberose, Bilke and I were clearly reaching the end of our endurance. I watched people die every day. I could see the timing of it in their eyes and in the way they developed a certain gait, which we knew as the death shuffle. Bilke and I constantly watched one another for these signs.

Then came a most memorable day, when two high-ranking SS officers were at the morning roll call. After the official count off, the officers took over.

"Attention," one of them said. "Sixty experienced machine-mechanics are needed for an important project. All those who qualify are to step out now."

About six hundred people stepped forward.

The SS men were overwhelmed and consulted with one another. After a moment, one addressed the crowd.

"All applicants will be tested. Those who do not qualify will be shot on the spot."

That was enough to thin the ranks considerably, but still about two hundred remained, among them Bilke and me.

Each prisoner was going to be tested for his skill as a mechanic, but, of course, they had no tools, so the test had to be oral.

The SS men set up two tables and split the group in half. We lined up single file about fifty feet behind the tables, several guards arrived to keep order, and the screening process began. Because of the gap between us and the tables, we couldn't overhear what was being asked. But behind each table, two groups formed, a small one of those chosen to go, and a much larger one of the unfortunates destined to remain.

My turn came before Bilke's. I went before the SS officer with a certain amount of confidence—since there were no tools, he couldn't prove my complete lack of mechanical skills. But my age was against me. In Germany it took years to train mechanics in apprenticeship programs. I stepped up to the table.

"Experience?" the SS man asked.

"Two years at the Steier-Daimler-Puch munitions factory in Radom, Poland, another year on the mechanic's team in Blizyn." I was grateful I could speak German fluently.

"How do you measure the circumference a circle?"

"Diameter multiplied by 3.14."

"Very good, over there." He pointed to the smaller group. I was accepted.

Next came Bilke's turn. I was a little uneasy after hearing the questions. Bilke was at least five years older than I and had apprenticed as a mechanic for most of his life. But he had little formal education. I had seen him take apart a broken sewing machine, locate the problem, and make new parts for it from scratch, but I didn't know if he could answer a technical question.

My fears proved well founded. Bilke was rejected and sent to the larger group.

When the process was completed, I dared to approach one of the SS men.

"Sir, forgive me, but you have rejected an excellent mechanic with uncommon skills." I pointed to Bilke, who was standing a bit outside the rejected group. When he saw me speak to the German, he knew that I was interceding on his behalf, and he waved to me.

"We have our quota," the SS man said. "Get in line."

"But he would be such a help—"

"Get in line now, before I shoot you and him and choose someone else."

I shut up and fell in line with the others. Within a few minutes, our numbers were noted, and the sixty of us were whisked out past the gates to a waiting truck. The two SS officers rode in a car in front of the truck and four guards in two motorcycles with sidecars, behind it.

I left Lieberose just in time to avert death by starvation, but there was no joy in it. I had left behind my best and only friend, my last link to the past. I could not imagine life without Bilke. I looked around the truck and realized I was among complete strangers for the first time since my ordeal began. Slowly I hung my head and cried.

Evidently, moving sixty ragged prisoners selected as experienced machine mechanics was an important war activity. Our small convoy of a truck, a car, and two motorcycles was not run on *Holzgas*, an inefficient substitute for gasoline, but on real petrol. In the traffic tie-ups that formed around downed bridges, blasted roads, and other results of incessant allied bombings, our small prisoner convoy was waved on by the German MPs ahead of other military vehicles. I wondered why we had become such an important asset when only hours before we were being deliberately starved to death. And why, if they wanted skilled mechanics, had they rejected Bilke? And most of all, what would happen to me when the Germans found out that I had lied about being an accomplished mechanic.

In the meantime, these fears were overridden by gratitude for the devastation I saw all around us. Although our truck was covered with a tarpaulin and we were ordered to sit crouched over with our heads between our legs, we nevertheless managed to see the tremendous destruction caused by Allied bombing. About two hours into the journey, we got off the main road and onto a secondary road full of bomb craters. On each side of the road, we saw wrecks of cars and trucks that had been hit and bulldozed off the road. Every time a wreck came into view, heads would raise a bit so that we could take in the scene, and there was a murmur of satisfaction and joy. The wrath of God was being unleashed against the Nazi murderers by American bombers during the day and the British at night.

Our tormentors were beginning to pay the price for their unspeakable crimes, but, of course, this was not enough to make us happy. It was about the beginning of January 1945, the middle of a ferocious winter. It was late afternoon, and we hadn't eaten all day. Between the cold and the hunger, we were approaching that twilight zone when the body refuses to obey orders because all the available energy is gone.

Finally the convoy pulled off the road into an isolated field. We were permitted to get down to relieve ourselves, but there was no food for us. The guards on the motorcycles ate their rations while the staff car trained its headlights on us, and the officers covered us with submachine guns. Finally, several men from the group went over to the officers and pleaded with them for something to eat. They told them that we hadn't eaten all day and that some of us might not make it through the night.

The officers became visibly agitated at this. The thought of bringing in fewer than the sixty prisoners they signed for must have been unnerving. After a short conference, they dispatched one of the guards on a motorcycle to a nearby farmhouse to see what he could fetch. The guard came back with the sidecar full of kohlrabies.

We lined up in the dark under the glare of the headlights, and each one of us got half a kohlrabi. Farmers feed the stuff to their pigs, but for us it was a feast.

Night fell and with it came a howling wind and bitter frost. The Germans decided to continue on and ordered us onto the truck, where we huddled together for body warmth. I was grateful for the warm overcoat Boris had given me and kept thinking of Bilke.

Soon I sank into a semiconscious delirium and had a recurring dream that had plagued me often. I saw my parents and my sister Bluma climbing a mountain made up of bundles of clothing. They were naked, holding their clothing in a neat bundle with the shoes tied together by the shoelaces. When they reached the top of the mountain, they each dropped their bundle where it belonged and began down the other side of the mountain. I tried to warn them that there was nothing but a burning pit at the bottom, but they couldn't hear me. The louder I screamed, the less audible my voice became.

Someone was shaking me awake. It was a young boy sitting next to me. I was in a cold sweat, and my throat was parched.

"Thank you," I said when I had regained my composure. "I couldn't go through that again. But I'm afraid you woke me from one nightmare into another one."

"We don't know that yet," he said. "Where could we go that is worse than Lieberose?"

He and I began to talk quietly. His name, he said, was Daniel, and he hailed from Bialystok. I asked him how he managed to pass the mechanic's test in Lieberose. He said he did it the same way I had—he answered several technical questions with answers he had learned in fifth grade. He was only sixteen and like myself was the only survivor of an extensive family.

Now that Bilke was gone, I needed a friend, and I took to this boy naturally. He responded in kind. We vowed to stay together and help each other. This encounter lifted my spirit, and a surge of new energy entered my body. We fell asleep huddled together for body warmth.

At dawn the convoy came to a halt, and we were once again ordered out of the truck, lined up, and counted off. The cold wind and the frost were numbing. I buried my head in the fur collar of my warm overcoat and again thanked Boris, my Birkenau savior. After the count off, we were turned over to two armed SS guards who signed for the delivery and took responsibility for us. As the sky lightened, we found that we had come to a concentration camp called Sachsenhausen.

Although we had arrived at our interim destination, our problems were not yet over. Because it was early morning, we were shunted aside to stand in the cold, completely exposed to the howling winds for more than two hours until all the ordinary work units marched out of camp to their assigned jobs. Daniel and I huddled together, wasted and worn to the bone. Each time a gust of wind blew, I thought it was the last I could withstand.

Finally a capo took notice of us and asked why we were standing out there. He then walked into the guardroom, got us a barrack assignment, took command of us, and marched us to the kitchen, where we each received a slice of bread and a quart of a hot coffee substitute. Afterwards, he marched us to our assigned barrack in a familiar Auschwitz-like setting.

Here again, while marching in this strange God-forsaken place, I heard someone call my name. I turned and there was Aamek Birenbaum, grinning with happiness because he spotted me. We exchanged a few words, and he promised to come to my barrack after roll call.

Aamek came to see me that evening before the barracks were locked for the night and brought me a piece of bread. God knows he needed the bread as badly as I did, but he insisted I take it. We talked at length about our experiences.

I asked about his mother, Salka, and whether she had accepted Davidek's death in Birkenau. He said he didn't think she ever would, even if she survived the war.

When it was time to part, I cried. Aamek was a link to my past, to a world that could never be again, regardless of the outcome of the war. I embraced him and bid him good-bye.

After lights out, I shared the piece of bread Aamek gave me with Daniel. I tried to tell Daniel about Aamek and what that encounter meant to me, but we were exhausted and soon fell asleep.

The next day our group of sixty was called out after the roll call and marched back to the entrance gate of the camp. Here two *Schupos*, German policemen noted for their two-visored caps, counted us off and signed for us. We fell in and began marching with one *Schupo* at the head of the column and the other in the rear.

A fresh sense of hope washed over me. The policemen were older people who looked like soft-hearted grandfathers, a far cry from the SS killers or the Ukrainian savages we were used to having as guards. As we marched, the civilians in the streets gave us furtive glances. They knew the war was lost and that there would be hell to pay for the treatment of the hollow-cheeked, gaunt-faced prisoners who now seemed to be everywhere.

For us, it was a strange experience to be among normal, everyday people, as if we had come back from purgatory to rejoin the human race. It was hard to reconcile what I saw on the Birkenau ramp with these normal-looking people going about their everyday tasks. How could these kind-looking, hard-working, gracious people have spawned so many monsters?

Soon we arrived at a railroad station. Our two *Schupo* guards didn't seem overly concerned with guarding us and rightly so. Where would we go? One of them leaned against a wall, keeping a lazy watch on us, while the other went to the ticket window and bought tickets for all of us, just as if we were normal people. Then they ordered us to sit in a small circle in an out-of-the-way corner of the station.

Because the guards appeared human and mild mannered, some of us began to talk with them. Amazingly, the guards listened to our concerns, which as always, were about food.

"What can we do?" one guard said. "They gave us money for this trip, but to buy food you need ration cards as well, and we don't have any."

Earlier we had noticed several nurses on the ramp dispensing sandwiches and coffee to wounded German soldiers on the way to or from hospitals or military men on furlough.

Now, one of us nodded to the nurses. "Couldn't you ask them for something?"

"They are only there for the soldiers. They wouldn't just give food to anyone."

"But surely, we would qualify," one of the prisoners said. "Aren't we going to a factory to help with the war effort?"

The *Schupos* were undecided, then another prisoner added, "Sir, it'll do no harm to ask, and we are so hungry."

Finally, one of them, grumbling a bit, went to speak to the nurses. We could see him negotiating with them. After a few minutes, we got sixty sandwiches and a bucket of sweet ersatz coffee. The sandwiches were small and barely touched our raging hunger, but somehow this human intercourse made us feel better. We expressed our gratitude to the *Schupos*, and they promised to try and get us food at every stop once we began our journey.

When our train was about to arrive, we lined up in twos at the far end of the platform. A regular passenger train pulled into the station, and the guards arranged to have the last car cleared of all passengers. Then the sixty of us took their place. The paint in the car was well worn, and the seats were plain wood, but it was a far cry from a cattle car. After having been treated like animals for years, it was a strange luxury to rejoin the human family.

It was also confusing. We stopped several times, and each time, the guards were true to their promise and got us as much food as they could. They were clearly simple, kind people doing an assigned job the best way they could. I had no way to understand their actions, because in my mind I had long ago consigned all Germans to hell.

At one point in the journey, I remember going into the toilet that was shared with the other cars and finding a crushed cigar butt in the ashtray. I grabbed it as if it were a fortune, and in the world of the camps, it may as well have been. It was still smoldering, and when I returned to my seat, I pulled on it until it was alight and took a deep puff. The world spun around me, and I started to gag. I handed the piece of cigar to Daniel. He put it out carefully and tucked it into his pocket.

That evening we arrived in Swinemunde, a port city on the Baltic. We disembarked and marched toward the sea, visible from a distance. The guards were a bit confused as to where we were supposed to go and had to ask the help of several passers-by before we finally arrived at the foot of a pier where a coal barge was tied up. After discussions with the captain of the barge, our guards ordered us on board. We went down into the bowels of the ship worried only about where our next meal was going to come from. Our guards assured us that they would go into town and fetch us some food, and soon they returned with some bread and margarine for supper. The next day the ship lifted anchor, and we sailed into the mist.

We knew that our destination was an island called Peenemunde, but we had no idea what sixty starved, worn-to-a-shadow wretches could do there to help the Nazi war effort. If our lives weren't on the line, the whole thing would have seemed like a comedy of errors.

After a short boat ride, we arrived at a pier and were lined up and counted off. At first when I looked about, it seemed that we had come straight to hell. As far as the eye could see there was nothing but heaps of rubble. Our guards marched us across the island, and the further we marched, the more thorough the devastation became. I was in awe at the power of the Allied bombing effort. The island had to have been carpet-bombed by hundreds of planes because even though there was enough rubble for a small city, the only thing still standing was an occasional charred facade. The Germans were finished, they had to be. The free world had risen to the challenge of a mad leader and a nation gone mad with him, and I knew that it was only a question of a little more time until they had their victory.

The familiar sight of guard towers and barbed-wire fences came into view.

CHAPTER 8

PEENEMUNDE
AND
LIBERATION

Having a pool of expendable prisoners available to do with as they pleased, the Nazis hatched many schemes that used the skills of the enslaved to further their chances to win the war. Medical experiments with humans were commonplace. Counterfeiters were in great demand as part of various plans to flood the world currency markets with perfect counterfeits. Artists who could forge paintings of old masters were sought out for much the same reason, and jewelers and dia-

181

mond cutters were highly prized. But once their assigned jobs were completed, most of these experts were eliminated to bury the secrets of their illicit work.

We had heard rumors of all of these schemes in the camps and assumed that we were at Peenemunde for some similar reason. But what possible purpose could sixty Jewish machine mechanics near to death by starvation serve in the German war game?

We marched into the camp in the afternoon sometime in the beginning of January 1945. Our faces were dirty from the soot of the coal barge, and we looked like scarecrows, ragged, hollow eyed, and spent. We lined up for the by-now-familiar routine of registration and then the *Lageraelteste*, the inmate head of the camp, surveyed the sorry-looking lot of us.

"All Jews?" he said.

One of the guards nodded. "I didn't think there were any of the swine left."

A harangue about camp rules and regulations followed. He told us that he liked his barracks clean and that infractions of the rules would be punished severely. He then added, as an afterthought, that we were supposed to be first-class machine mechanics.

"And you'll have to prove yourselves in the factories," he said, "or else, you are dead."

I kept close to Daniel. We were there under false pretenses and needed to stick together as much as possible.

The campelder then told us that we would be sent to different barracks and asked if there were juveniles among us. Daniel grabbed my hand, and the two of us stepped out. We were assigned to the youth room, a special room in one of the barracks.

The blockeldest of the barrack to which we were assigned, a German national wearing the green triangle of a convicted criminal, took us to our room and showed us to our bunks. When we saw the youth room, we could see that the campelder was serious about his cleanliness. The room looked like German military quarters. Each bunk was made up neat as a matchbox. The real wooden floor was scrubbed clean like the deck of a ship. And the walls were covered with signs emphasizing the value of cleanliness and listing the punishments for nonadherence to the rules.

There was no one in the room, so Daniel thought of the piece of cigar I had picked up in the washroom ashtray on the train. He had wrapped it carefully in newspaper and then put it in a stringed bag around his neck. When he got a chance, he used his small penknife to chop the cigar into small pieces so it looked like tobacco.

Now he took his priceless gift to the blockeldest. The blockeldest immediately got some thin paper, rolled a cigarette, and lit up. When he inhaled he began to cough, then to nod and smile. He motioned us to follow him to a locker in his room and gave us each a hefty slice of bread. He also told us to clean up in the washroom and rest on our bunks until roll call.

"You know," he said, "you were lucky to be assigned to the youth room. You'll get a little better treatment than the rest."

We ate the bread slowly, swallowing each morsel with mouth-watering pleasure. Each bite meant new strength and hope. After we finished, we fell into an exhausted sleep.

We awoke when the others came back from work. They were mostly children, some as young as ten or eleven and all Gentile Poles and Russians. We were glad to see them because they didn't look badly undernourished and also because they did not ask if we were Jewish. We told them we were Poles and that was enough. The new *Sachsenhausen* numbers on our tunics didn't reveal our Jewish identity.

We went out to our first roll call hoping against hope that we would buy time here until the end of the war.

At the roll call, I could see that the inmate population at Peenemunde, about a thousand prisoners, was primarily Russian POWs with a sprinkling of Gentile Poles and Gypsies. Except for the sixty newcomers, I could see no other Jews in the camp. I also examined the prisoners for the telltale signs of starvation and prisoner mistreatment. To my relief, everyone seemed relatively healthy.

Then a large group of prisoners marched into the camp semicircle and dumped ten or twelve bodies from handdrawn wheelbarrows. The bodies were almost naked and frozen stiff.

I leaned over to the boy next to me. "Where did they come from?"

"From the commando that shovels the snow at the airfield," he said. "Every day, the prisoners who can't do anything else are sent out to keep the runways open. The runways are right on the sea, so every day they bring back a dozen or more. If you want to live, don't ever get on that commando."

"How do I avoid it?" I asked.

"You make sure you are useful elsewhere. But you don't have to worry. You are a mechanic."

After the roll call, soup and bread were distributed in the barracks. The juveniles got extra portions of soup and bread that evening. One of the rooms was punished for some infraction of the rules, and their food was given to us.

The next day we lined up for morning roll call under brilliant camp lights in cold so penetrating that my feet were numb within minutes. The SS camp commander, tall and handsome in a leather coat lined with fur, accepted the count off and other reports. He then asked for the sixty newcomers to step out. Daniel and I stepped out and joined the others.

The commandant gave us a little speech, telling us of the importance of the work on which we were about to embark. We were to help build a weapon of terror that would finally bring Germany's enemies to their knees: the V-2 guided missile. He ended his speech with the usual warning: "Perform or you will die."

The sixty newcomers joined a large commando of several hundred workers, with four capos and four guards assigned to the group. All of us lined up in marching order and were counted off as we passed the gate. We marched to a rail station and boarded a train that took us directly underground to the factories. We made several stops and at each stop a group of prisoners got off, taking some of the sixty along. My turn came on the third stop.

The capo counted off ten newcomers to go along with about forty of the old workers. Daniel and I separated. Since neither of us were mechanics, we decided the night before that it wouldn't be smart to be in the same group.

My work unit, headed by a Russian capo named Sasha, entered a tremendous, underground workshop with hundreds of machines humming noisily in two rows. In the center of the hall was a narrow-gauge rail line on which raw materi-

186 / JOSEPH HORN

als and finished products were transported to other factory locations on small hand-pumped carts. The hall extended as far as the eye could see.

There were different sections, each separated by a glass-enclosed room raised about two feet off the floor. This was evidently the control room of the section where the department manager worked. It was in front of this room that Capo Sasha directed our group.

An elderly man came out. He was dressed in suit and tie with a gray overgarment. Pinned to the lapel of his coat was an identity card with his picture and his title prominently displayed. He looked drawn and tired with a soft grandfatherly way about him.

"Herr Kindt," Capo Sasha said, "the ten additional workers you requested have arrived."

Capo Sasha ordered us to step out, and Kindt looked us over. His eyes rested on me.

"Very good," he said. "Take the group to the plant foreman, all but this one." He pointed at me.

As soon as the group left, he led me over to a workbench, took a piece of metal, and clamped it in a vise. He then handed me a file. "Put a flat surface on this for me."

I took the file in my hands, but Herr Kindt could clearly see them trembling. Before now, the most complicated mechanic's task I had ever done was to operate a drilling machine on an assembly line. I scraped the file across the rough metal several times, lifting it to see if I was making any difference. After a minute or so of this, Herr Kindt laid his hand gently on mine.

"You are not a mechanic, are you?" he said.

I shook my head.

"I thought not. I am afraid I cannot use you. I'll have to ask the capo not to bring you back tomorrow."

I broke down and cried.

Herr Kindt shook me. "Here, stop that."

I lifted my head, and I saw in his eyes that I had touched his soul.

"Don't be afraid," he said. "They will find other work for you in camp."

"But please, Sir, that's what I'm afraid of. If you reject me, they'll send me to the airfield. I won't last a week there."

"Don't be foolish. They can't send you outdoors to work in this weather."

"But they do. The prisoners shovel the snow off the runways. I've seen them bring back the dead in wheelbarrows. Please, it will kill me."

"This can't be true," he said, then looked at me again, started walking, and motioned me to follow him. He took me to the next department, muttering all the way, and told the engineer there what I had told him. They asked me questions about conditions in the camp. I told them I was Jewish and therefore likely to be punished more severely.

After more discussion, they took me to a corner behind some idle machinery where there was a four-wheeled cart with several small barrels of different kinds of lubricants on its bed. They explained to me that my job would be to pull the cart across both departments and fill the lubricant reservoirs of all the machines. They showed me where the different drums of lubricants were stored and wished me luck.

I thanked them, and above all, I thanked God for saving my life one more time—and this time by, of all people, two Germans.

The Peenemunde concentration camp was run according to all the rules and regulations that prevailed at the time in Nazi Germany. It was not a death camp, and in fact until my arrival, no Jews had ever set foot on the island. But the conditions under which the camp inmates toiled were so atrocious that it was easily one of the worst living hells in Hitler's dominion.

The awful savagery of the camp became apparent to me as I listened to the tales of the children in my room. Almost every night, one or another of the children would be dragged from their bunks and sexually abused by the green triangle German capos. These children, mostly Russians and Gypsies, would return in the morning in a state of shock. Then they had to join everyone on the roll call and go out on the assigned job to do a day's work under horrible conditions.

The green triangles, the convicted German criminals whom the Germans used as capos, held absolute sway over the camp, and their code of ethics prevailed. Complainers or troublemakers were found in the washrooms in the morning beaten to death or drowned in the washbasins.

Like many other camps, Peenemunde had a hospital on the grounds with about twenty beds lined up in two rows in a long, freshly painted hall. The floor was scrubbed clean, and there was a side cabinet next to each bed. The beds were covered with snow-white linen and invitingly puffed feather pillows and covers. There were nurses on duty. I never saw a cleaner hospital room. But to the best of my knowledge, the hospital never had an inmate patient in the beds. Anyone who needed help beyond a dab of iodine or an aspirin was dispatched quickly with an overdose of phenobarbital.

Daniel and I learned the ropes quickly and shared any extra food either of us managed to "organize." Daniel got a job dispensing precious gasoline at a pump in the underground factories—the Germans didn't trust one of their own with the job. He would sometimes get a tip in the form of a cigarette, which we later exchanged for food. My job with Herr Kindt was good. When I wasn't keeping the machines lubricated, he would send me on errands to different sections of the underground factories. I learned where the German dining rooms were located and, though I was strictly forbidden to enter, I would rummage through the garbage pails left outside for pickup. Occasionally, I would find a half-eaten sandwich or a crust of old bread. I would bring such treasure back to the youth room and share them on the bunk with Daniel. Also, Herr Kindt would sometimes come back from lunch and seemingly absent-minded leave his mess kit on the workbench. That was a sign for me to take what was in it. Mostly, his lunch was boiled, unpeeled potatoes. Food was scarce even for the German workers at such an important facility.

Eventually I asked Herr Kindt to bring the peels from the potatoes he and the others had eaten, thinking that I could extract some food from them, but the Germans were as thorough and efficient at peeling potatoes as at anything else and left little to scavenge. Still I took the potato peelings back to the barrack and managed to exchange them with the Russians for bread. The Russians had no compunctions. They toasted the potato peelings on the stove and ate them with pleasure.

Daniel and I were holding our own. We were constantly hungry, all our efforts were centered on food, our bodies were emaciated, but we weren't falling back. This was mostly because we spent most of our days indoors protected from the fury of the ferocious winter outside.

In the meantime, the group of mechanics that came with us to Peenemunde was getting smaller each day. Some were rejected on their jobs and sent to shovel snow on the airfield. Others became sick. Still others were found dead in the washrooms, victims of the routine brutality of the green triangles. After about four weeks at Peenemunde, there was no one left alive from the group of sixty except Daniel and me.

By this time, our Jewish identity was entirely forgotten. Nobody knew, nobody cared. We were finally freed from the long-held fear that the Nazis would never let any Jew survive the war. We were now fighting for sheer survival as equals among all the other victims of Nazism. Daniel and I discussed this repeatedly at night to bolster our spirits. We thought we might be the only Jews still alive in the camps, which gave us incentive to fight on.

Then came the day Herr Kindt did not show up for work. Later that day a replacement was sent from another section. The new man was a harsh-looking, no-nonsense German who reminded me of Nell from Blizyn. I simply tried to stay out of his way. Capo Sasha noticed the change and knew that I had lost my benefactor. I felt that my days on the job were numbered.

On the third day of Herr Kindt's absence, it happened. Capo Sasha pulled me out of the ranks in the morning after roll call and exchanged me for a Russian boy of the airfield commando. It happened so quickly, I didn't have time to signal Daniel.

I was being sent to work on the airfield. It was my death sentence. It would only be a matter of time.

The airfield was right at the edge of the sea, and during the night, the winds swept the snow into dunes several feet high. When we arrived in the morning, it was impossible to tell where the runways were. The capos staked out an area of about a square mile in the snow and put poles with red flags in each corner. There were two guards with us. We were told that anyone going beyond the staked-out area would be shot. Then we fetched shovels from a tool shack and began shoveling.

My first day on the job was worse than anything I had imagined. We were completely exposed. There was nowhere to hide from the terrible gusts blowing in straight from the Arctic. A Russian boy standing next to me gave me a couple of rags to tie around my hands so they wouldn't freeze. My coat was a life saver, and the fur collar helped to keep my ears and head covered. My feet were like icicles, and I kept thumping as I worked to keep them from freezing.

People all around me were coughing, a hollow sound that seemed to come from the deepest recesses of their lungs. Some were spitting blood, cursing the day they were born, cursing the north wind that bent us double every time it blew.

The capos wore woolen scarves around their faces and fur-lined gloves on their hands. The guards were dressed in greatcoats and warm leather boots. Under their helmets they wore scarves wrapped around their entire faces leaving just the eyes exposed.

There were several other work units on the airfield, each one assigned a different job. One of the luckier ones worked on airplane maintenance with German mechanics in underground hangars that shielded them from the winds. There was also a camouflage commando that covered the few planes that braved the winds and ice to take off and land. But the snow-shoveling commando was a kind of catchall that took all prisoners who were not assigned to other jobs. For this job there were always vacancies.

When it was time to go back to camp after the first day, at least a dozen men had succumbed to the cold. I was given the task of loading one of the bodies on the wheelbarrow I brought that morning for that purpose. The body was naked, because as soon as someone fell, the others would pounce on him and get the rags and shoes off his body. In all my years in the camps, I had never seen such callous, brutal behavior.

Daniel gave me all of his soup that night. He did it to bolster my spirits as well as to help my body fight the cold. I thanked him but told him it was of no use.

"My friend," I said, "I am at a dead end. There is no way out of it."

"No, don't say that," Daniel said. "You have a good overcoat with a fur collar, and you never know what will happen. Perhaps the wind will subside."

"Right, perhaps the Messiah will come."

"Please, Yossek, don't give up. You won't leave me to be the last survivor."

The next day, Daniel brought me a large sturdy paper bag that he got somewhere at work. It was a double-strength cement bag. I strapped it under my tunic to help ward off the wind.

I went to work for several more days, and each day I trudged the wheelbarrow to work in the morning and brought back a naked cadaver at night.

I slept only fitfully. My short life kept spinning in and out of dreams, blurred images of my parents, my two brothers, and my sister Bluma. I longed to join them.

One day when we lined up in the morning, a Gypsy capo named Arno took a long look at me when he handed me the wheelbarrow. With his experienced eye, he must have been able to see I was not long for this world, because when we got to the airfield, he brought up one of his proteges and ordered me to change coats with him. I gave up the beautiful warm overcoat with the fur collar that Boris had risked his life to give me in Auschwitz and put on the rag they threw at me in exchange. I knew then I wasn't going to make it until the end of the day.

The wind was so ferocious, it was impossible to breathe. I needed to cough but couldn't because it hurt whenever my chest expanded. I didn't have the strength to work, but I couldn't stand idle so I walked over to the nearest guard and asked permission to relieve myself. As I walked to the spot near the red-flagged pole designated for this purpose, I made a decision. Better to be shot by the guard than become a frozen cadaver. When I reached the red flag that marked the end of the perimeter, I kept walking.

My heart thumped, and I was barely able to trudge in the snow. But the wind had subsided somewhat. I waited for the shot in peace, my mind focused on my mother's face. I wanted her to be my last image.

I heard yelling. At first I couldn't make out what it was then realized the guard was screaming, "Stop or I'll shoot!" I kept walking and held my head high so as to give him an

easy target. I didn't want to be injured. I couldn't stand any
more pain.

The yelling stopped. No shots were fired. I kept walking.

After a while, I heard footsteps behind me. I turned and
saw the guard trudging through the snow in my direction,
his rifle slung over his shoulder. I stopped, then turned back
towards him. Soon we were face to face alone in the field
of snow. He was a man in his late fifties and seemed very
upset.

"You didn't shoot," I said in German.

"I never killed anyone yet, and I am not going to start
with you," he said. "What did you think you were doing?
Where were you going to go?"

"Only to my grave."

"But why?"

I shrugged. "Look around. Better a bullet in my head than
slow death in the wind."

He nodded then took my arm.

"Look, you'll get no bullet from me. Now come on, I'll
do what I can to help."

Together we trudged back in the snow.

"Where did you learn such good German?" he said.

"I am Jewish, so it was easy for me because the languages
were similar." I told him about the capo who removed me
from my job in the factory and the capo who robbed me of
my coat.

"*Schweinerei*," he said, then told me he was regular
army, not SS. A shopkeeper. He was drafted late in the war.

When we got back to the work area, he let me go into
the tool shack to warm up. When it was time to return to
camp, he told the capo to let someone else push the wheel-

barrow. On the way back, he walked next to me and kept an eye on me.

When we got to camp, he reported my escape attempt at the guardhouse and was ordered to escort me to the *schneiderstube* (tailor room) to have a target sewn on the back of my coat. He was also ordered to remain in camp until roll call to report the escape attempt to the camp commandant.

As we entered the tailor room, the two tailors, elderly German nationals with the red triangles of political prisoners, stood at attention. The guard explained the situation to them and became visibly angry when he got to the part where I had been robbed of my coat.

"So how could I shoot him in cold blood?" he said. "I knew he wasn't trying to escape. Where would he escape to off this island and in this weather?"

They then discussed how to report this incident to the commandant so that no one got in very much trouble.

I kept quiet.

Events had overtaken my emotions to the point where I was in a vacuum. I had decided to end my life, and now had three Germans trying to help save it. I must have looked so pathetic that even in this abode of the damned there were people whose virtue I could still touch.

But rules had to be obeyed, and one of the tailors began sewing a ready-made target, about ten square inches, printed in bright red on a white background, to the back of my coat. All prisoners who were deemed prone to escape had to wear such targets.

Next came the fateful roll call.

After the count off, the commandant asked as usual if there were any reports to be made. The guard dutifully reported the escape incident, and I was told to step out. The commandant looked over my pathetic, wasted, barely living figure.

"Where did you want to go?" he said.

Before I could say anything, one of the tailors stepped out and asked permission to speak. He seemed at ease with the commandant, as if he knew him well. He told him of the *schweinerei* of Capo Sasha in removing me from an important job in the plant and replacing me with one of his cronies. He also told how airfield Capo Arno had robbed me of my coat. The commandant listened attentively, then ordered the two capos to step out.

"Arno," he said, "fetch the crony who has this man's coat."

Arno ordered the man to step out, and again we exchanged coats. Then the commandant walked up to Arno and slapped him twice, hard.

"Any more incidents like this," he said, "and you will join your charges at shoveling snow. Sasha!"

Capo Sasha snapped to an even more rigid attention.

"Take this man back to his old job tomorrow and make damned sure nothing happens to him in the interim or else you'll be shoveling snow, too."

He dismissed us all with an expansive gesture.

I couldn't move. I could not believe that a place like Peenemunde could look so good in the dead of winter. My life was given back to me by forces stranger than any fiction.

That night when I joined Daniel on the bunk, we cried and embraced. Again he gave me some of his food to build me up, then I fell back on the bunk in total exhaustion. My last thought before I fell asleep was that my mother had to be watching over me.

Production of the V-2 rocket continued on the island of Peen-emunde until the middle of February 1945. Daniel and I continued to work in the underground factories, hoping each day that the next day would bring an end to the war. The German workers who commuted daily from the mainland were convinced that the end of the war was near. After all, despite Goebbels, they knew the truth, that the V-2 could not make an appreciable difference on the battlefield and that the Nazis were doomed.

Germany was at the edge of an abyss. They had committed such unspeakable crimes against humanity that it was impossible for them to consider surrender. Those who knew of the atrocities (and most did) couldn't imagine facing the wrath of their enemies, especially after the whole truth of the atrocities became known. They were especially wary of the Russians against whom the most terrible crimes were committed. So when their leaders implored them to fight to the last man, they were willing to do so.

For Daniel and myself, the collapse of the Third Reich meant the final phase of our six-year ordeal. Our desire to survive was greater than ever before. The stakes were so much higher. We really believed that no Jews could have possibly survived what each of us had gone through. That meant that we alone were left to shout from the rooftops the horrors that were perpetrated upon us, our families and our people.

The daily routine at Peenemunde allowed me to build up my strength somewhat. I worked at my old job as distributor of lubricants for two machine sections. Herr Kindt came back on the job after a severe illness, and I was able to get extra food through him as well as from Daniel. Daniel's job of dispensing petrol proved to be more and more lucrative as he was able to trade extra fuel for food. At night each of us brought whatever we could scavenge and ate with enormous relish.

One night when we returned from work, there was a great commotion in camp. We quickly heard that at high noon, a small work commando of Russians charged with camouflaging the planes on the airfield had overwhelmed their guard, piled into an airplane, and took off on a snowy runway. The Russian front was not far away, and the Germans were frantic because the secret of their underground factories was now out.

At first we were told we would all be shot in retaliation.

At roll call that night, the commandant announced that every tenth prisoner would be counted off and shot in the morning. No one slept that night, not only because of the threat of execution, but because we expected a night raid of a thousand bombers to blow away the whole island. But the night passed uneventfully and in the morning, no one was shot. The next day Russian planes appeared over the island, and there was an air-raid alarm for the first time in months, but again no bombs fell.

Shortly thereafter orders came to begin the evacuation of the island. No one was harmed in retaliation for the escape.

The inmates of the Peenemunde concentration camp were to be the first to go. We were loaded onto a coal barge and taken to Swinemunde on the mainland. After several days, they put us in freight cars.

And then began the final, unforgettable, horrendous, pre-liberation journey.

For the next four weeks, the Peenemunde group criss-crossed Germany or what was left of it. On many occasions, we were strafed by Allied planes and took heavy casualties. But so did the German troop trains that always seemed to be near us.

On several occasions, we were dumped into concentration camps—Ohrdruf, Bart, Nordhausen, Erlich, Dora—for a few days and then reloaded into other cattle-car trains to be shuttled back and forth in the collapsing Reich. At one camp, an American fighter plane would appear each morning and circle overhead until the roll call was over and all the inmates were returned to the huts. It was as if his mission was to safeguard us, and that gave us hope. But the Nazis took us all out one night, forced-marched us to a nearby town, and loaded us on yet another freight train for another dreadful journey.

There were plenty of opportunities to escape, but where to? German kids, twelve to sixteen years old who had enlisted in the *Volksturm*, a last ditch defense effort, became the monitors for the Gestapo. These kids, soaked in Nazi propaganda, ruled the streets. Anyone who could not provide them with acceptable travel orders, they hung without trial. They set up dragnets for German army deserters. It was a very common sight to see bodies of men swinging from lampposts with signs on them saying, "I am a traitor."

The country was in chaos. The incessant bombing and strafing by the Allies put such fear into these supermen that they became supercowards. When the trains were strafed, the guards were the first to run away as far and as fast as their legs would take them.

In those last days of the war, I witnessed such terrible atrocities committed by Germans as well as by inmates against each other, that to this day I can barely write about them.

Finally, on the first of April, our freight train pulled alongside a ramp, and the doors were opened on a vista of distant, peaceful villages, gentle farmland, and rows of fruit trees. The farms were well tended, and the farmhouses looked prosperous.

If that wasn't wonder enough, when we lined up and began marching, we passed a group of Jews marching in the opposite direction. Some were dressed in the traditional Jewish garb, others in normal civilian clothing with the Jewish yellow stars.

Daniel and I could only stare while others among us said things like, "Look who's here. They got away from the gas."

We marched on and soon came to the entrance of an evacuated state-of the-art military base called Bergen. The base was built during the war to accommodate the best of Hitler's military units, an elite SS panzer division, as well as a panzer-training school. At the entrance was a large painting of a German Tiger tank with the flags of the unit stationed there.

We came to a square that looked like a military parade ground surrounded by a complex of eight buildings. Six of the eight were dormitories facing each other on the long side of the square, and the other two completing the rectangle were administrative offices and cafeterias. All eight buildings were built of cement, two stories high with slate red roofs. I could see that the entire camp was made up of several such complexes joined by wide boulevards that ran through clean, neat grounds.

The Peenemunde group was moved into one of the dormitories. Rolls of concertina wire with their razor-sharp barbs were tossed around the perimeter, and armed guards were placed at fifty-meter intervals. Guards were also placed on the roofs of each of the eight buildings.

We entered these new accommodations in total amazement. The beds were actually equipped with spring mattresses and covered with white linen. The blankets were made of soft wool. The washrooms were tiled, and there were real mirrors in them. The corridors were wide and the floors polished.

The former occupants, whoever they were, had left in a great hurry. Personal things such as socks, underwear, shaving cups and brushes, letters and pictures were strewn about the floors. In one room, I saw an open safe with millions of reichsmarks in neat packages—now just so much toilet paper. Another room was strewn with helmets, rubber rain gear, and other military articles.

In our group discipline was gone. The SS who accompanied the Peenemunde unit throughout the journey disappeared. The guards surrounding us and on the building roofs were Hungarian soldiers who we later found out had enlisted in Hungary to train with the German panzer division. The capos had lost their authority, there were no blockeldests, and everyone just grabbed a bed and occupied it.

When the excitement of settling down in the lap of luxury abated, we began to wonder who was going to feed us? And when? And where? Only about half of the original

Peenemunde group had survived the forced marches, Allied dive bombers, and the brutality of some of the guards, and the survivors were ready to kill for a slice of bread.

No one suspected that we might be Jewish, but being Polish in a roomful of Russians under those circumstances was just as dangerous—Poles and Russians in the camps were notoriously hostile toward each other. Still, as long as we possessed nothing of value, we were left alone.

In the evening, there was no roll call. The Hungarians simply brought a kettle of soup from the kitchen to each occupied building and distributed it under the supervision of an armed SS man who wore a white armband, we guessed, as a sign of surrender. At night the prisoners were left to their own devices.

Several capos were beaten to death that night, now that they had lost the protection of the Germans. Others, who seemed to have many defenders, were just beaten senseless. A new regime of caveman justice took over, the strongest lording it over those who were weaker. For Daniel and me, this was one more hurdle to jump over on the way to that day of days when the liberators would finally come.

Nothing happened for a few days. The weather was good, but hunger still threatened to rob us of our lives at this last, most critical moment. The more hungry the Russians were, the more dangerous they became. If anyone had anything edible in his possession, he was immediately robbed, if not killed.

One of the cross-buildings of the complex housed the kitchen as well as the food storage rooms in the basement. Each day prisoners would make a run across about fifty feet of open space for a basement window behind some bushes, slide down into the food storage area, and come out with their shirts and pants loaded with potatoes and vegetables. After the first few raids, the Hungarian guards on the roofs began shooting at the perpetrators. A couple of Russian boys were killed and several wounded, but the deadly game continued.

About ten days after our arrival in Bergen, I decided that unless Daniel and I secured some food somehow, the six longest years anyone ever had to endure would have been in vain. So we studied that basement window and all the access and escape routes from it. We also timed the changing of the guards on the rooftops and came up with a plan that might work.

Daniel and I made our way to a clump of bushes closest to the window and waited until ten o'clock when the guards were due to change. When we saw the relief guards approaching, I made a zigzag run across the exposed area. A volley of shots rang out, and bullets whizzed by me, but I made it safely across. Previous visitors had shattered the window and bent back the bars. I slid easily down into the basement, my heart pounding.

After I got used to the darkness, I could make out bunches of carrots, potatoes in bushels, and bins full of some kind of radishes. I ate a carrot while I loaded my shirt with carrots and potatoes. I had also drawn strings around my pant legs so I could stuff my pants up to the waist. When I was sufficiently loaded, I jumped up, grabbed hold of the bars, and pulled myself up and out through the window.

I had to make the deadly run through the gauntlet again, but now I was loaded down and wouldn't be able to sprint as fast. I looked up at the guards from behind the safety of the bushes. Their rifles were at the ready. They knew I was in there and waited for me to come out. I couldn't wait too long, because someone might come after me from inside the building. I paused, chewing on my carrot, thinking it might be my last meal.

Then I heard the most beautiful sound ever. The air-raid sirens.

A few moments later, a trio of American planes appeared overhead. The guards scurried off the roofs, and I made it across to Daniel and safety.

When we walked into our dormitory, the eyes of all the Russians were immediately upon us. We made it safely to the bunks. I threw our treasure on the bed and immediately took some potatoes and carrots to the corner where several Russian boys were lying about. I had picked up Russian years earlier and by now could speak it with fluency. I told them that this food would help us all until we were liberated. This was enough to buy us protection from the others, and Daniel and I were left alone to eat in peace.

Two days later—on April 15, 1945, at 9:15 a.m.—I heard a commotion downstairs. I walked over to the open window to see what was happening. Daniel was embracing a soldier. A Russian boy was kneeling and kissing the hand of another soldier. Both of these soldiers were dressed in khaki and in the background was an armored vehicle with a five-pointed white star on its hood.

The Allies had arrived.

My knees buckled. I barely made it to my bunk. Resting my elbows on my knees, I held my head in my hands. I no longer cared about food. I knew I would never crawl again. Questions kept popping into my head. Who am I? What am I? Where am I? Is anyone left of my family? Will there be a life as I once knew it?

Eventually I pulled myself together and went downstairs. British soldiers were all over the camp dispensing crackers and a milklike substance. They were fumigating people with DDT.

Then, from the administrative building, the Russians dragged out the body of an SS man they had beaten to death. I came closer and saw the grotesque-looking body still twitching, dressed in the hated uniform.

Strangely, I found my need for revenge had already left me.

At that moment, I wished for nothing more than a return to normalcy so I could find out if any members of my family were alive. It was as if a part of nature, which had steeled me for survival, had now abandoned me. Different rules would now prevail. It was going to be a new world, a new beginning, a new life with different values. I was newly born.

With the English I had learned in Miss Soboll's clandestine school, I asked a British officer about the state of the war.

"The Nazis kaput" was his answer. Those were the sweetest words I heard in all my life.

"Have you liberated any Jews? Were any Jews left alive?"

He told me that he had just come from a nearby concentration camp in a place called Belsen where there were many Jewish survivors. He then took me to his Jeep and gave me several cans of conserved meat.

Daniel had also gotten some food from the soldiers, and we had a liberation feast. But our camp immunities no longer worked, and for the next two weeks, we were sick with dysentery and spent most of the time in a makeshift hospital.

The real shock of liberation came a few days after I got out of the hospital, when the Polish survivors of Bergen arranged a liberation ball. I walked into the hall dressed in jacket and slacks obtained from the Red Cross, feeling like a human being for the first time in years. The band was playing a song called *"Chryzantemy Zlociste,"* or "Golden Chrysanthemums."

At that point, the memory of my experiences clashed with the unlimited possibilities of my future, and just as in Ella Psherover's room in the small ghetto, my legs below the knees went numb. I grabbed a chair and barely managed to sit down.

A pretty girl noticed and came over to me. "Hi, I am Renia. Are you all right?"

"I think so," I said. "It's just that this is all...it's so *much.*"

She sat down next to me. "I know," she said. "I'm Jewish, too, but I survived the war with my mother by pretending to be Polish Catholics. We worked on a farm not far from here. I thought we were the only Jews who made it."

"I know the feeling. My name is Yossek, and I am so very happy to meet you and..."

I was still struggling to express my feelings when she threw her hands around my neck.

"Never mind that now. We're young, and we're strong. And we have a new life to live. Come on let's dance."

And so we danced that night. Oh, how we danced.

CHAPTER 9

AFTERMATH

Of all my family, I am the only survivor.

My father, Judah, was a master at the art of making a deal. He managed to not only do well under the heavy anti-Semitism that existed before the war but also to use his skills to help his family survive in the ghettos until that survival was no longer possible. The principles I learned from him about choosing your contacts carefully, finding a way to keep all sides of the deal happy, and maintaining your integrity enabled me to stay alive by smuggling in both Blizyn and Auschwitz. My father died in Treblinka.

My mother Yohevet's drive to see her children succeed gave me the heart I needed to continue to live. So often, when

I felt that the suffering was more than I could bear, I thought of her no-nonsense resolve to see her children thrive in the world. And on that day on the airfield at Peenemunde, when my life was saved by the miraculous compassion of a German guard, I know she was watching over me. She, too, died at Treblinka.

My oldest brother, Abram, was the intellectual achiever of the family, graduating at the top of his class and yearning to find a way to apply his skills in mathematics and science. He eventually escaped to Russia where he faced starvation and exposure just so he could live free. He was recaptured when the Germans overran Russia in 1941, and I never heard from him again. I have long given up hope that he survived.

My sister Bluma was both beautiful and gentle. Her hair was jet black, her eyes deep brown, and her face became freckled in the summer in a way that made her look mischievous. What I remember most were the times when she talked with her teenaged friends, mostly about boys. I was four years younger, and the boy/girl relationship was a complete mystery to me, so I would have loved to listen in, but I was always chased out of earshot. My parents were able to protect Bluma throughout the ordeal of the ghetto, and for that I am grateful. Perhaps the most courageous of us all, she chose to accompany them to Treblinka.

My brother Eli had fire in his soul. He stood up to the rabbis when the regimentation became unbearable and got us both kicked out of the cheder. He stood up to the pogroms before the war, and he refused to bow even to his Nazi tormentors. In the middle of 1943, at the munitions factory in Radom, he turned on a particularly cruel Polish foreman and beat him severely. The guards pulled Eli off the foreman, dragged him outside, and bullwhipped him to within an inch of his life. He was then thrown into a bunker, tortured, and executed a few days later.

I last saw my father's two brothers, Uncle Hershel and Uncle Aron-Meyer, as broken and beaten men in the small ghetto at Radom. I am sure they did not survive long afterward. My cousin Harry (Anoosh), one of the soccer-playing twins, who saved my life at the deportation *aktion* in the small ghetto, survived as did his twin brother Abram (Mumek).

It was by sheer chance that I learned the truth about my cousin Abram, Uncle Hershel's son who was one of the sixty workers who helped make the mysterious straw mats in the last days of the Radom ghetto. A few weeks after the sixty workers disappeared, a boy named Fishman, who was in charge of the decontamination of clothing at Blizyn, recognized his brother's bloody and bullet-ridden jacket in a shipment of clothes to be repaired and cleaned. The brother had been one of the mat makers and had left a note in the jacket pocket that explained what happened.

Once the workers had made enough mats, they were put to work reopening all the mass graves in the area and burning the bodies. At the time, German propaganda was making good use of the discovery of mass graves of Polish officers slaughtered by the Russians in the Katyn forest. The Nazis didn't want to leave similar mass graves behind them. The mats were to erect a wall around the graves to shield the work from onlookers. Once the mass graves were cleared out, the mat makers were themselves killed and the bodies stripped and burned.

Nearly everyone whom I knew growing up in Radom also disappeared without a trace. Miss Soboll, who fostered such a sense of camaraderie among her students. Rabbi Chaim, who risked his life to officiate at my Bar Mitzvah. My friend Lustig, who escaped to Warsaw with his family but was never heard from again. And hundreds of others who were simply friends and neighbors. An entire society is now gone.

Moniek Ackerman, my smuggling friend from the ghetto, did manage to escape with his parents, two sisters, Celia and Rose, and their husbands to Warsaw. There they lived for a time disguised as Aryans with Rose, who looked the most Aryan, acting as liaison with the outside world. One evening, on her way back home from her job, Rose saw a military cap reflected in the light of the family's apartment window. She ducked into a doorway across the street and watched as the Gestapo brought the entire family down to a truck waiting at the curb.

Moniek made a break for it. One of the Gestapo agents knelt and brought him down with several shots. Only Rose survived to tell me the story later.

Ella Psherover's sacrifice in staying behind in the ghetto was not in vain. Her mother and sister were eventually shipped to the concentration camps, but they survived to liberation. I saw Mrs. Psherover occasionally in the displaced persons camps after the war but soon learned to avoid her. I reminded her of Ella, and every time she saw me she burst into tears.

Of those who were in the camps with me, there are also many whom I never saw or heard from again. One of these was Boris, Bilke's sauna friend at Auschwitz, who risked his life many times in order to save ours. Another was Bilke himself. I don't believe the SS carried out the threat to shoot those who failed the mechanics' test at Lieberose, but I also don't believe Bilke could have survived much longer in those conditions. Basia Greenshpan, the beautiful girl who's broken leg was miraculously set by a German doctor in Birkenau is alive and well.

Stempel, Reuben, Jan the radio announcer, and so many more simply vanished. They were probably consumed by the flames of the Holocaust, but I do not know for sure because no one who does know has survived.

Also, because of the confusion of the war's end and the Cold War's beginning, I was never able to learn the fate of the few blessed Gentiles who helped me. I hope that Wanda, Herr Kindt, Capo Janek, the guard at the airfield, the tailors at Peenemunde, even the *Schupos* who cared for us in transit all survived and prospered, but I will probably never know.

Daniel recovered from his dysentery after liberation. Quite soon he found a brother in one of the liberated camps in the area, and the three of us lived together for a while. They became extremely religious, joined a group of Orthodox, and were among the first to leave the camp for Palestine.

Several weeks after my liberation, I heard someone call me by my childhood name as I walked the streets of Bergen-Belsen. I turned and saw Danka Lastman, who had once walked Till, the Abwehr officer's Dalmatian, and later had been part of the all-night discussions with Moniek, Lustig, and me in the small ghetto.

Danka told me of her family. Her parents were killed in the so-called "*aktion* of the intellectuals" in March of 1943. The Germans asked the ghetto administration to compile a list of prominent people to exchange for important German POWs. When the list was completed, the people were turned over to the SS, who robbed them and executed them in a nearby cemetery.

Danka's older brother, Mendel, was deported to a work camp but later escaped with four other boys into a nearby forest, where they were killed by Polish partisans who were fighting against the Nazis—exactly the fate Wanda had once warned me of.

All four of Danka's sisters survived. One of them, Tosia, was sent to the death camp at Maidanek but survived to be shipped to Bergen-Belsen and later liberated. Danka and the other three were sent to work in an ammunition factory in Pionki, where Danka sorted and packed gunpowder.

Salka Birenbaum and her son Aamek survived. Not only that but her husband, Motek, came back from Siberia in 1945. They found one another in postwar Radom and resumed a family life. Salka gave birth to another son in June of 1947, and the family emigrated to the United States in 1949. There Motek died of a heart attack in 1973, never once having asked what happened to Davidek.

Salka still lives with her children and grandchildren. When I ask her what she remembers most of her wartime experiences, she tells of the day she found Aamek after the war. He was in a Polish orphanage near Warsaw, asleep in bed when she was brought to his room. She sat down on the bed and gently shook him awake. He opened his eyes, looked at her, then threw his arms around her. The first thing he said was, "Mother, I survived, but not once did I lick the soup kettle."

In 1952, after I had established myself in business in New York, I got a call from Long Branch, New Jersey. It was Sol Mincberg, who had saved my life at least twice in Blizyn and whom Bilke and I had saved in Auschwitz. He had emigrated to the United States and was now working as a factory manager. I was able to help him establish his business and so pay back some of the kindness he'd shown me earlier. We spent a lot of time together, but we never talked about our days in Blizyn. Sol died of a heart attack at age forty-two. Few people felt his loss as keenly as I did.

Dr. Weinapel, who once stood up to Nell in order to save his patients' lives, survived the war and later emigrated to Ellenville, New York. There he set up a small practice with his wife and nurse, Saba, and spent his leisure time painting scenes of Blizyn as he remembered it. I saw him several times over the years, and he even treated one of my daughters for a minor problem when we were on vacation in the Catskills. Dr. Weinapel died of cancer several years ago, but Saba still exhibits his paintings at Holocaust libraries around the country.

Of course, not all those who survived the war were its victims. In 1967 the German Consul in New York informed me that hearings were to be conducted at the consulate the following year to examine charges against a man who was an SS officer in Radom during the Nazi occupation. My name came up, among others, as a possible witness.

The man was Paul Nell.

In 1968, I told what I knew about Nell to several judges and prosecutors who came to the United States for that purpose. Then, in 1972, I was asked to go to Hamburg at the court's expense to testify at Nell's trial.

I arrived in there on a Sunday afternoon in 1973 and took a taxi from the airport to the hotel where a room was reserved for me. I tried to relax in the backseat of the taxi, but I began to tremble at the thought of facing a man who once said I lived or died at his discretion and nearly proved it by making me dig my own grave. I calmed myself by remembering Jacob's final cry of "I must live, I must tell," before Nell put a bullet in his brain. I had lived. Now, at last, I would tell.

Arriving at the hotel was a bewildering experience. Everyone around me spoke German, but they were all so pleasant and courteous, and I was used to hearing German from inhuman monsters. Something felt wrong, and that feeling kept me on edge. I retired to my room early, emotionally drained, but sleep was impossible. Presently, I dressed and went down to the hotel restaurant for dinner. Again, the restaurant was full of pleasant Germans enjoying their Sunday meal with a lot of laughter and *gemutlichkeit*. I hardly ate. Finally, I decided to go for a walk.

As I started down the hotel steps, I came face to face with Nell.

Although I knew him instantly, I don't think he recognized me—after all, he never knew the Jews under his control as individual human beings. But he knew I was the one who had come to testify against him. He could tell from my clothes that I was an American, and he knew the court used this hotel to house the witnesses.

His eyes met mine for a split second, then he turned on his heels and walked down the street. The first thing that came to mind was a fantasy that had haunted me for years. I come face to face with Nell, unlimber my machine gun, point it at his belly, and unload the entire clip. But I had no machine gun, and my feet seemed stuck to the ground. All I could do was watch his familiar gait from behind. I almost expected to see his dog.

I was on the edge of fainting, but I made it back to the lobby and asked the hotel clerk to connect me with the Hamburg Jewish Center—the authorities in New York had given me the number in case I had any problems. I found someone there, and he agreed to meet me in my room just a few minutes later.

Almost before he closed the door, I grabbed his sleeve. "Why is this brutal mass murderer allowed to walk the streets?"

He led me over to a chair, talking quietly. "You must understand, the courts are reluctant to try these cases. Prosecution of war criminals is not popular."

"Popular! Do you know what this man is?"

"Yes, but the German public wants to bury the past. Most Germans believe that all armies commit atrocities, and that they're just being singled out for punishment because they lost the war."

I sank down in the chair, speechless. This was the first time I had come up against the denial of the truth. "But...yes, atrocities are sometimes committed during a war, but the Holocaust had nothing to do with war. It was an act...a horror...it was..."

"I know, and this is why Nell is being tried. The Hamburg authorities have been working for the last ten years to bring a case against him. But the political realities right now are that they have to let him live freely on a low bail." He patted my shoulder. "Don't worry, we will see justice done."

The trial took place as scheduled. There were three judges, a prosecutor, and two defense attorneys flanking Nell in the courtroom. There was also a jury of Nell's peers. I was the only witness. I took the oath on a Hebrew Bible in English and gave my testimony in clear, precise English. I speak German fluently, but I would not utter one word of German while I was there.

And I told. I told them of the anonymous Jewish man who had dug his own grave at the carpenter's shop on

Szkolna Street in Radom. I told them of Jacob, whose blood had spattered my clothes because Nell needed an example. I told of the hospital full of sick prisoners Nell had ordered killed because it was easier than caring for them.

I told of Dudek Schatz.

Schatz came to Blizyn with the original eighty Jews from Radom. He was a tall handsome man in his early thirties and was assigned a job as the manager of the food storage room. Needless to say, this was the best job in the camp. He had a girlfriend named Sally who had lived in our building in Radom, whom I knew well. They were a lovely and loving couple.

Inevitably, someone accused Schatz of pilfering. That day, at the evening roll call, Nell motioned to Schatz to step out, put his pistol to his forehead, and shot him without uttering a word. Sally ran out, fell on her lover's body and begged Nell to kill her also. Nell patted his dog, then turned and walked away.

I also told of Martofel.

After the ten-man work detail led by a prisoner auxiliary had escaped from Blizyn by faking orders from Nell, Nell ordered that another auxiliary had to die as retribution. Sol Mincberg was told to choose the victim.

I was working in the auxiliary's hut at the time and overheard the agonizing discussion about who should be sent to die. In the end, the nine remaining auxiliaries decided to draw lots. It was then that Martofel, who came from a cultured, well-to-do family in Radom, announced that he wanted to volunteer. He said that he was forty years old, by far the oldest of the auxiliaries, and was contemplating suicide anyway.

At the evening roll call, Stempel and I helped Martofel dig his grave while all three thousand brothers and sisters stood at attention. When we were done, Martofel handed me his pince-nez and told me to give them to someone who might need them. He then said good-bye and laid down face up in the grave, where Nell shot him in the head.

Nell was convicted of crimes against humanity and murder. He was sentenced to life imprisonment. I went back home to my life in America, a million light years away from Germany and Nell.

About six months later, I received another letter from the German Consul in New York. Nell's defense had located Sergeant Zlotosz, the SS man from Szkolna Street. They were granted a new trial with Zlotosz as a corroborating witness. The second trial took place in the same Hamburg court presided over by the same judges. This time I asked my wife to accompany me, knowing that I needed the emotional support. But the second trial was only a formality, ending as soon as Zlotosz took the stand and confirmed what I had said.

In 1989 I attended a meeting of prosecutors of war criminals from all over the world. At a coffee break, I found the prosecutor from Germany and asked her if she had heard of the Nell trial. It turned out she was from the Hamburg prosecutor's office and was familiar with the case.

"And Nell?" I asked. "What became of him?"

"He is still in prison," she said. "He's made several appeals for leniency over the years, but they've all been denied."

Then she looked me straight in the eye. "If I and my colleagues have anything to say about it, he will stay there until he dies. Some of us do know the truth."

Because I have survived the Holocaust, I am often called on to try to explain it to people who don't believe it. I'm not merely talking about the neo-Nazis or political conservatives who claim the Holocaust was merely Jewish propaganda, that it couldn't possibly have been as bad as it is portrayed. Such people have a pathological need to believe what they believe and will never be swayed by facts. But there are many sensitive thoughtful people who simply can't comprehend what happened.

In 1980, I was part of a panel of Holocaust survivors and representatives of the media to discuss how the media handled matters pertaining to the Holocaust.

At one point in the discussion, Gabe Pressman, a television reporter, said, "Of course, had I been there, I would have grabbed a submachine gun and taken a bunch of them with me."

When my turn came, I said, "Gabe, as we are sitting here, you and I, I don't feel a discernible difference between us. We are both Jews of the same age and generation. But I was there and you were not."

I then told him of the incident in Blizyn when I was marching behind Nell with a shovel in my hand to dig my own grave. I assured Gabe that I was young, I was strong, I had already lost my family, and I was certainly no coward. I could easily have killed Nell. But I knew that if I did every last prisoner in the camp would have been executed, and so I was prepared to walk to my death. In many ways, that was the harder decision. I then asked Gabe what he would do.

Gabe apologized, but I'm not sure he was convinced.

Since that time, I have put a great deal of thought into why the Jewish community didn't offer the kind of resistance

Gabe was talking about when faced with genocide. In hindsight I can see several reasons.

For one thing, the Holocaust took place at a time when
the hatred of Jews had spread throughout Europe to such an
extent that German anti-Semitism was simply the best orga-
nized. The prejudice underlying the Holocaust was certainly
as strong in Poland and the Ukraine as it was in Germany.
Indeed, my father's generation remembered the Germans of
World War I as being more enlightened than the Poles, and
as Wanda had warned us, the Polish resistance routinely shot
escaped Jews on sight.

Even America had an active fascist party before the war.
Political conservatives were preaching anti-Semitism from
the floor of Congress. And during the war, the Allies viewed
the extermination of the Jews as an internal affair of the
Axis governments and did nothing to intervene. There was
resistance in the Warsaw ghetto, but it received no support
from the people outside. If Jews had tried to organize resistance, they would have literally been fighting alone against
the world.

Also, the Holocaust was the capstone of generations of
grinding persecution. Our fathers, our grandfathers, our
great-grandfathers for generations had lived through random
violence and routine injustice. And they believed that the
best way to survive was to support one another rather than
fight back. Rabbinic leaders taught that *Etzba Elochim*,
God's finger, ruled the world and that nothing happened
unless it was ordained. Jews were told they should accept
their hardships, struggle on the best way they could, and wait
patiently for the Messiah.

At the same time, my generation was beginning to doubt
this counsel. Militant Zionism was born during the thirties,

and many of us began to dream of a Jewish state where we could finally defend ourselves. The rabbis fought against this new activism because they believed that God alone could bring the Jews back to the land of Israel, and He would do it by a miracle, not by force and hard work. So the Holocaust caught the Jewish community at a time when it was divided, with the old leaders losing their credibility and a new leadership not yet in place.

But the thing that made the Holocaust so hard to fight against was the nature of the Holocaust itself. For one thing, it was such a huge injustice that it was almost impossible to believe, even in the face of direct evidence. Jacob had escaped from Treblinka, and his family would not believe what he had seen with his own eyes. Many Hungarian-Jews in Auschwitz died because that was easier than accepting the reality of what went on around them. The horror of the Holocaust was easy to deny simply because it was such a horror.

Also, the planners of the Holocaust did everything possible to encourage this need to deny the truth. The Holocaust came on gradually, with the ghettos forming in stages and the Gestapo and SS taking only select groups at first. Also, the Nazis spread rumors that deported Jews were simply being sent to the Ukraine to till the land. The deportation trains from western Europe were well appointed, and deportees were allowed to take their personal possessions. The Nazis even built that model camp at Thereisienstadt with streets and individual huts and humane conditions. They encouraged inmates there to write letters back to their families, then once the word was out, the inmates were shipped to the real death camps. As a result, most of those who arrived in Auschwitz did not know what it was until they were marched into the gas chambers.

In short, everything was done to offer people hope when there was no hope. And this, combined with the memories of the Germans as a civilized people, the rampant anti-Semitism of the age, the generations of training in passivity, and the lack of clear leadership in the Jewish community, made it possible for the Germans to murder more than six million Jews with hardly a protest.

Some today wish to forget the Holocaust in the interests of healing.

In 1989, my wife and I, Sol (Aamek) Birenbaum and his wife Lynn, visited Auschwitz. We toured the first camp, Auschwitz I, where non-Jewish German prisoners were kept. We traveled around with the crowds, listening to a Polish guide talk about the martyrdom of Rev. Maxymilian Kolbe, a prewar anti-Semite who had recently been canonized by the pope. The guide hardly mentioned Jewish suffering.

Later I traveled the three kilometers to Birkenau, or Auschwitz II, where the true genocide took place. The Germans had dynamited the gas chambers and crematoria before they left, but the remains are still preserved. This was the place where two million Jews, more than half of them children, died simply because they were Jewish. It was nearly deserted.

There is a terrific pressure on those who remember the Holocaust to universalize the event—to expand it to include the others who suffered under the Nazis. It is felt that, by continuing to hold the Holocaust up as an example of exclusively Jewish suffering, we are perpetuating a cycle of hatred that needs to be ended.

I can understand this feeling, but I don't agree with it. Many other groups—Gypsies, homosexuals, prisoners of war, political opponents of all kinds—did suffer and die under the

Nazis, but the coldest, most efficient horror was reserved for the Jews. No other group was so systematically hunted down. No other group was so relentlessly and routinely persecuted. No other group was driven so close to complete eradication. As Elie Wiesel has put it, "Not all victims were Jews, but all Jews were victims."

And surely we cannot heal the wounds the Holocaust has left by denying that it happened. Indeed, it is the people who are most interested in denying the Holocaust who are most likely to repeat it. The best way to keep the world safe for Jews and all minorities to live in peace is to remember the past clearly. Otherwise, it could happen again all too easily.

Many have asked me where God was during the Holocaust, and to that I have no answer. I can only say that I did not see Him at Auschwitz, and I have heard no reasonable explanations of where He was since then.

Some Orthodox Jews believe that God sent the Holocaust to punish His people for their sins. They point out that assimilation among Jews had reached unparalleled proportions, especially in Germany just before the advent of the Nazis. Just as God has, according to some, sent the AIDS epidemic to punish homosexuals for their behavior, so He sent the Holocaust to punish Jews for their secularism. The Holocaust was a slap in the face by an angry Father to a wayward child.

We in the camps felt differently. There were many who continued praying and believing in Him even as they saw their mothers and children killed. I think they believed that the Holocaust was an aberration and that God's ultimate judgment would not be wrong. Most of us believed strongly in the traditions of our heritage—they were the mortar that held us together—but were disenchanted with our religion.

We certainly didn't feel that we had done anything to deserve the punishment we received.

And yet there were things that happened in the camps that can only be described as miracles. In spite of the perverse brutality and official savagery, sparks of humanity existed. There were always some good people touched by a Godly spirit who found the strength to withstand the evil and risk themselves to help another.

And perhaps there is one more word I can say on this subject.

When I saw Danka Lastman in Bergen after the war, the sight was a revelation to me. I still thought of her as a young kid, trailing after that huge dog, or a fellow sufferer talking low over a table in the middle of the night. But now she was a woman, full-grown and astonishingly beautiful. She had her whole life ahead of her, and so did I.

Danka and I were married in the United States on November 20, 1949. We named our first born daughter Sandra Joy, after our mothers Sara and Yohevet. Our second daughter was named Bonnie Judith, after my sister Bluma and my father Judah. Our third daughter, Ellen Mae, was named after my brother Eli and Danka's sister Manya.

And this is the right place to finish my story. The Holocaust changed my life irrevocably, but it did not end it. I have done more than survive, I have also lived and continue to live.

Perhaps this is the best sign that the human spirit is truly Godly.